FAITH
OF OUR
SONS

FAITH
OF OUR
SONS

A Father's Wartime Diary

FRANK SCHAEFFER

CARROLL & GRAF PUBLISHERS
NEW YORK

FAITH OF OUR SONS
A Father's Wartime Diary

Carroll & Graf Publishers
An Imprint of Avalon Publishing Group Inc.
245 West 17th Street
New York, NY 10011

Copyright © 2004 by Frank Schaeffer

First Carroll & Graf edition 2004

Library of Congress Cataloging-in-Publication Data is available.

ISBN: 0-7867-1322-4

Printed in the United States of America
Interior design by Simon M. Sullivan
Distributed by Publishers Group West

This book is dedicated to . . .

Corporal Matthew Commons, Army Airborne Ranger, A Company,
1st Battalion, 75th Ranger Regiment, killed serving his country
on March 4, 2002 . . .

Staff Sergeant Shane Henry Kimmett, Air Intelligence Agency, Air Force
Special Operations Command, killed serving his country on August 7,
2002 . . .

Second Lieutenant (Therrel) Shane Childers, USMC, 1st Battalion, 5th
Marines, killed serving his country on March 21, 2003 . . .

Staff Sergeant Aaron White, USMC, Medium Helicopter Squadron 364
MAG 39 3rd MAW Purple Foxes killed serving his country
on May 19, 2003 . . .

. . . and their families.

"Greater love hath no man than this. . . ."

1

Diary of Deployment

February 17, 2003 [First Entry]

John called. He said he will be deployed! I'm elated for my boy because he sounds happy. I'm elated in the same way one is "elated" by looking over a cliff. Adrenaline and terror also surge.

We are about to go to war in Iraq and are already at war in Afghanistan. John could have sat out the action at a desk. I asked him if he volunteered for this mission.

"Yes, I did, but don't tell anyone."

"You mean Mom?"

"Yes. She'll be really upset if she knows I volunteered."

"I won't tell."

"What do you think, Dad?"

"I'm proud of you, and scared. What about you?"

"I'm excited and nervous," said John. I could hear the excitement, not the nervousness, as he added, "I'll be doing special weapons training. You know, sort of a refresher course to get ready; all very cool!"

I wanted to say the right thing. I did not know what that was.

"Well, do all you can to stay in touch while you're over there," I said lamely.

"I will, but remember, no news is good news. If something happens they'll let you know within twenty-four hours or so."

"When shall I tell Mom?" I asked.

"Wait till it's one hundred percent sure I'm going."

"What is it now?"

"About ninety-nine percent."

———————

After she woke up from a late afternoon nap Genie and I made love. She suggested it and I decided to wait till afterward to tell her. As I took her into my arms I thought, Genie, you don't know it yet, but this is your last carefree moment for a long while.

Mine was a sadly absentminded effort. I still did not tell her when we were done and lay side by side holding hands.

———————

I hid behind my cooking, fixing a late lunch: a mozzarella, avocado, and poached egg salad. I drank wine, though I usually wait till dinner. I wanted Genie to enjoy her meal in peace. If she noticed that I ate a very small portion, she didn't say anything. I told her after she was finished eating. I did say he volunteered. I can't keep secrets from Genie. She nodded and held my hand. She did not cry. We sat quietly for a moment. I felt as if I'd explode.

John, forgive me for breaking a promise.

———————

Genie was calm throughout the evening as I hovered around her. I was afraid to be alone. Her lovely eyes sparkled with tears from time to time. But her voice was steady as she said, "This is what he trained for. He'll have to do this so he knows that it's all been worth it."

"You're so calm about it." I said in a shaky voice. "Don't you feel scared?"

"Yes."

"But you don't seem emotional about it."

"Darling," said Genie, as she draped an arm around my shoulder, "I think you have enough emotion for the both of us."

———————

11:29 PM. Genie is asleep now. I'm sitting at my computer looking for comfort in my writer's routine, telling this page what I can't speak. I will not be able to tell my friends who do not have sons and daughters in the military about John's being deployed, at least not for a few days. I won't titillate them with John's service. To them this will only be gossip about someone else's bizarre misfortune. I'll only tell Cathy and Danny Boucher—our friends who live close by who have both sons in the Marines. And I'll e-mail some of the military parents who've been writing to me. To them it will not be like gawking at a traffic accident. I pray John is not killed.

2

Background

A father will fight for his son. In the night my weapon is prayer. In the day, those of us who are writers sometimes fight for our loved ones with words.

> From: Fannie Zollicoffer
> Monday, November 25, 2002 3:39 PM
> To: Frank Schaeffer
> Subject: Your edited piece
>   Dear Mr. Schaeffer,
>   Below is the edited version of your column for tomorrow's *Washington Post*. Please look it over and let me know if you'd like to make any changes.
>   Thanks,
>   Fannie Zollicoffer

The Washington Post, November 26, 2002
My Heart on the Line
By Frank Schaeffer

Before my son became a Marine, I never thought much about who was defending me. Now when I read of the war on terrorism or the coming conflict in Iraq, it cuts to my heart. When I see a picture of a member of our military who has been killed, I read his or her name very carefully. Sometimes I cry.

In 1999, when the barrel-chested Marine recruiter showed up in dress blues and bedazzled my son John, I did not stand in the way. John was headstrong, and he seemed to understand these stern, clean men with straight backs and flawless uniforms. I did not. I live on the Volvo-driving, higher education–worshipping North Shore of Boston. I write novels for a living. I have never served in the military.

It had been hard enough sending my two older children off to Georgetown and New York University. John's enlisting was unexpected, so deeply unsettling. I did not relish the prospect of answering the question, "So where is John going to college?" from the parents who were itching to tell me all about how their son or daughter was going to Harvard. At the private high school John attended, no other students were going into the military.

"But aren't the Marines terribly Southern?" asked one perplexed mother while standing next to me at the brunch following graduation. "What a waste, he was such a good student," said another parent. One parent (a professor at a nearby and rather famous university) spoke up at a school meeting and suggested that the school should "carefully evaluate what went wrong."

When John graduated from three months of boot camp on Parris Island, 3,000 parents and friends were on the parade deck stands. We parents and our Marines were not only of many races but were representative of many economic classes as well. Many were poor. Some arrived crammed in the backs of pickups, others by bus. John told me that a lot of parents could not afford the trip.

We parents were white and Native American. We were Hispanic, Arab and African American and Asian. We were former

Marines wearing the scars of battle, or at least baseball caps emblazoned with battles' names. We were Southern whites from Nashville and skinheads from New Jersey and black kids from Cleveland wearing ghetto rags, and big white ex-cons with ham-hock forearms defaced by jailhouse tattoos. We would not have been mistaken for the educated and well-heeled parents gathered on the lawns of John's private school a half-year before.

After graduation one new Marine told John, "Before I was a Marine, if I had ever seen you on my block I would've probably killed you just because you were standing there." This was a serious statement from one of John's good friends, an African American ex-gang member from Detroit who, as John said, "would die for me now, just like I'd die for him."

My son has connected me to my country in a way that I was too selfish and insular to experience before. I feel closer to the waitress at our local diner than to some of my oldest friends. She has two sons in the Corps. They are facing the same dangers as my boy. When the guy who fixes my car asks me how John is doing I know he means it. His younger brother is in the Navy.

Why were I and the other parents at my son's private school so surprised by his choice? During World War II, the sons and daughters of the most powerful and educated families did their bit. If the immorality of the Vietnam War was the only reason those lucky enough to go to college dodged the draft, why did we not encourage our children to volunteer for military service once that war was done?

Have we wealthy and educated Americans all become pacifists? Is the world a safe place? Or have we just gotten used to having somebody else defend us? What is the future of our democracy when the sons and daughters of the janitors at our elite universities are far more likely to be put in harm's way than are any of the students whose dorms their parents clean?

I feel shame because it took my son's joining the Marine Corps to make me take notice of who is defending me. I feel hope because perhaps my son is part of a future "greatest generation." As the storm clouds of war gather, at least I know that I can look the men and women in uniform in the eye. My son is one of them. He is the best I have to offer. He is my heart.

Ten years ago I would have laughed in disbelief if told I'd be flying a small American flag on my gate. That was before John and I wrote a book together, *Keeping Faith: A Father-Son Story About Love and the United States Marine Corps*. That was before he was about to be deployed into harm's way.

After his graduation from boot camp and then while being trained for his military intelligence job, stuck for a year in Fort Huachuca, Arizona, waiting for his security clearance, John found the time to write his half of our book. We finished it on September 10, 2001.

3

February 17, 2003 [continued]

I would argue with Genie but don't dare. We are both too fragile to risk a big cloud-clearing brawl, a sorry state of affairs for a couple known to stun and amaze children and friends with bouts of storming on an operatic scale.

To behave normally takes an act of the will, and normal behavior is indeed an act right now. I feel as if I'm peering out of a cage as the world passes by, a cage others can't see, yet one in which I've been corralled, condemned to pace alone. Old friends go their merry ways. I watch. To passersby I may appear as if I am one of them, but I'm not. I am only pretending to be in the world around me, but my mind, heart, and soul are with my son, hovering over him, a phantom of anxiety unable to do more than beg unseen powers to protect him.

Genie is by my side. She tries to comfort, but it is a case of the blind leading the blind. Jessica and Francis [John's older sister and brother] do their best to help. But they, too, are caught up in a web of anxiety over their "little" brother.

"I was flipping channels," someone wrote recently, "when I saw this tall young man in dress blues. I stopped and watched. I didn't even know what the program was. It turned out you were reading from your book on C-SPAN's *Book TV*. Anyway, I stopped and watched when I saw those Blues. . . ."

I doubt the viewer would have paused if she had just seen me. It was John she stopped for. In his dress blues, he looks like a six-foot-four-inch poster boy for the Marines.

But John has a real job, so I'm the one who answers the mail. It has come flooding in since that *Post* op-ed ran, not to mention all the TV shows they had us on. While promoting our book, during those weeks at the end of the year, John's being a Marine felt like a lark. But the fun ended with a sock in the stomach—war.

Yesterday I spent another five or six hours responding to the e-mail. So far I've gotten over two thousand messages, another thirty or forty just yesterday. A few weeks ago I complained to Genie, "How can I answer them all?" But now night after night—usually at two in the morning—I find myself back at my computer, reading and answering each message. I'm beginning to think that I need my new correspondents a lot more than they need me.

Saturday, December 07, 2002 11:45 PM
To: Frank Schaeffer

I just wanted to welcome you—belated, I realize—to the real world of the armed forces. . . . I am a career newspaperman, a 1971 U.S. Army veteran of Vietnam, where I served as a first lieutenant and the last Vietnam-era commanding officer of the 5th Public Information Detachment at Nha Trang (II Corps headquarters). . . .

My wife, Sylvia (an elementary school teacher), and I have four sons—all of whom wound up in uniform. . . . Sylvia and I were at all their basic training graduations—as well as at Zak's final jump and "graduation" from Airborne School at Fort Benning, GA, where earlier he had completed the last week of basic training with a fractured foot—and never complained until the week was over because he didn't want to fall behind his "battle buddies."

We went to Parris Island twice—for Jonas, then for Jon. Each time, our emotions ran as high as the American flag fluttering atop the pole on the mini–Iwo Jima Memorial at the south end of the bleachers. . . . And while we are full of pride in our four young men, we also are full of trepidation as we pray every day that Jonas and Zak stay out of harm's way—understanding that in the end, no matter what, God's will be done. . . .

Sincerely,
Kent Cockson

Tuesday, February 18, 2003 3:49 PM

I have two sons in the military (US Army), both either deployed or on their way. We differ, however, in that I am a member of a military family. But we are all kindred spirits.

My husband is retired from the US Air Force. My father . . . was a veteran of WWII, Korea, and Vietnam. He retired in January 1967, following 22 years of service. I am also a veteran, having served in the US Air Force. I have had a family member in the military serve in every conflict that this country has ever seen.

My two sons are 21 and 19, and the best I can do is to send them forth to follow the path they have chosen for themselves, and quietly shed my tears, sometimes when they aren't looking, and sometimes when they are.

When I left my younger son at Ft. Bragg, just days before he deployed, I hugged him and cried on his shoulder. Had he died, I don't know that my heart could have hurt any more. . . .

Nancy M. Dickinson

Tuesday, November 26, 2002 3:12 PM

Like your son, I have a foot in two worlds. I joined the Marine Corps a few months after graduating from one of those private schools for the "well-heeled." That was 22 years ago.

Since then I have spent 15 years on active duty and another seven in the reserves (and counting). While my parents were not exactly happy to see me join the Marines, they soon experienced a sort of awakening . . . so much so, in fact, that when I left active duty to attend a rather famous university, my mother questioned whether I was doing the right thing.

. . .

The beautiful irony of the Marine Corps is that it is the most inclusive "elite" institution imaginable. We who are Marines—or who have family members in the Corps—know that special bond that exists among people willing to make great sacrifices.

This, of course, makes the professor's condescending plea for an evaluation of "what went wrong" [quoted in the *Washington Post* op-ed] almost laughable. Maybe if his son joined the Corps, he would have a different point of view. Nonetheless, his remarks suggest not only the widening of the gap between the "protectors" and the "protected" but also a belief that such a gap is a good thing. . . . The strength of our democracy depends upon everybody having "skin in the game. . . ."

Semper Fi,
John Lowry

Sunday, December 01, 2002 11:01 PM

My husband and I [have] just returned home after seeing our youngest son Joe off on his return flight to the Air Force Academy in Colorado Springs after Thanksgiving leave. . . . Our older two sons graduated from Georgetown University where they received an excellent education. . . . When Joe announced over dinner last fall that a career in the Air Force was his first choice, I asked him his reasons. Without hesitation, he responded, "If others are willing to do it, why not me?"

. . .

Joe is not loving his experience at the Academy, but he is "appreciating" the physical and academic rigors which instill a profound respect for the uniform. . . . As Joe describes it: "Mom, we all eat the same food, do the same push-ups, crawl through the same mud, lack the same amount of sleep. No one cares what size house anyone else goes home to. We all just have to work together to survive."
Joanne Hurley
Visalia, California

Monday, December 02, 2002 4:16 PM
. . . Today, some patriotic fervor has been lost. . . . There are still some who berate the Vietnam generation, forgetting that most . . . went and proudly did what was required of them. We, my generation, march alongside of those men on Veterans Day all across this nation. . . . I am sure that our young men and women will be just as valorous now as the "Greatest Generation" was almost sixty years past. . . .
Gerald M. Rosenthal
Army Air Corps, 1941–1945

Tuesday, December 03, 2002 3:27 PM
When I joined the Marine Corps during Vietnam I could not understand [my dad's] worry or concerns, especially since he was a Captain in WWII. Now that I am the dad with a son about to go in harm's way, it is a different viewpoint. . . . I question our reasons for the war about to be started. [But] I am a patriot and believe in our country! When I was in the Corps, it was just me. At that age I was still immortal. Of course I came home a disabled veteran, which disproved that theory. . . .

If we go to war I will support America 100%. I may disagree, but I am proud that my son is serving. . . .

Sincerely,

Michael R. Kirby

P.S. Please tell your son *"Semper Fi."*

Tuesday, December 03, 2002 9:55 PM

I am in my twentieth year of service in the Marine Corps. . . . Regardless of how many years your son decides to serve he will always remain a Marine and that will be a common thread between your Corporal and the many thousands of others who have been Marines. It will be a title that he carries for the rest of his life. . . . You can be proud. . . .

To you and your son,

Semper Fi

Steve Clark

Lt. Col., USMC

Tuesday, December 10, 2002 8:57 PM

I fear for my son's safety as I'm sure you fear for your son's. . . . In your essay on the *NewsHour,* [with Jim Lehrer] you pointed out how some parents at your son's high school graduation asked "what went wrong?" I hope you responded that nothing went wrong—everything went right—and yes—the Marines are southern, thank goodness. (I was born and live in New Jersey.) At least they have the belief that they are protecting the weak from the crazed. Many people in our society do not appreciate how lucky we are. The service of your son, my son, and countless others is what allows the rest of us to sleep peacefully in our beds at night.

Sincerely,

Jon MacIvor

Friday, April 04, 2003 8:39 AM

In 1974, I was a smart-assed, tough little girl who thought she was a woman. While my family wasn't poor, they were working class. I would be the first to go to college. . . . Being an artist/poet hippie child, I was stunned [when I learned there was no money for college]. Having no concept of how to get money for school—no high school counselor enlightened me about scholarships—I joined the Marines. . . . I later heard the Marines referred to, while living in Boston, as "New Hampshire's blue collar road to college."

The surprise was that I loved it. I still use the leadership skills I learned. When I got out, I married a former Marine. A few years later while I was in art school, I learned he had a brain tumor. . . .

I transferred to another school, got a "real" degree in biology, put my art on a shelf and worked 60 hours a week to pay for all the medical treatments. He died and left me shell-shocked with $75K in medical debts. I lost my home. . . .

I remember sitting at the funeral on a very hot Virginia August day wondering how I was going to survive this. I closed my eyes and walked into a closet I kept in the back of my mind and slowly . . . pulled out my Dress Blues and pulled them on. Suddenly, my back straightened, my jaw stopped quivering and I sat calmly and with as much dignity as I could muster. I was even able to smile as I realized that this new National Cemetery at Quantico, Virginia, was built in an area popular to Marines for "necking." . . .

I am trying to hold all my debilitating memories at bay; the war is so good at opening Pandora's box. . . . Your son and all my brothers and sisters are in my prayers.

Semper Fi,
Christine Desrosiers-Naugle
The Fewer, the Prouder, the Women Marines

Friday, April 04, 2003 11:28 AM

We're probably about the same age. . . . I got drafted and did 11 months in Vietnam with the 101st Airborne as a rifleman. I got slightly wounded and sent home. I never gave the war another thought until the Gulf War started in '90. That seemed to stir up everything. The Internet, a few years later, has allowed many of us to reconnect, not just guys who did the same thing, but guys from your own platoon, your own squads. It has been a revelation. . . .

What made me want to write you is that they are still the same guys. Older, heavier, and bald, but still a group of men I am so very proud to associate with. That they number me among them as a full member is something I cherish. I wanted to tell your son that in 30 years the men he cares for now will still be the type who would do anything for him. They will still want to keep him covered in a fight, even if the fight is now with a zoning board or bill collector.

There are guys in our company who became wealthy and successful and guys who, until we found them, were sleeping under bridges. Doesn't matter. They're in the club. Watching my friend Roger, now a retired PhD, talk with a guy who'd have trouble spelling "PhD" was a joy. Their conversation from 34 years ago picked up seamlessly as they updated their stories. It was something I put off for years, maybe a residue of the '70s, maybe we all weren't ready for this, but it was wonderful to be among them again.

Your brave son will find this part of his life as satisfying and rewarding as any moment he has ever spent. I pray for his safe return. . . .

Thanks for listening,

Larry Kirby

Wednesday, December 11, 2002 4:35 PM

My son, SSGT Shane Henry Kimmett, enlisted in the Air Force in March of 1993. . . . He applied for and was accepted into the Air Force Special Operations in 2001. On August 7, 2002, at about 7pm he was killed when his Combat Talon II slammed into the mountains of Puerto Rico during a training mission. Shane had flown 260 sorties in two years. He was very proud to be a member of the Air Force and the elite unit in which he served. He was a member of the Air Intelligence Agency and the Air Force Special Operations Command. He was stationed at Hurlburt Field.

. . .

He had a great sense of humor, a big heart, and, most importantly, a true sense of what it meant to be an American. I will miss him for the rest of my life. It tore my heart out of my chest and reduced me to tears, tears that have not stopped falling since his death. I am proud of my son and what he stood for but I miss him terribly every day. I would trade places with him at a moment's notice. He was the best of the best.

I wish your son a safe tour of duty. I dread the impending war and have very mixed feelings about waging the war. However, I will support President Bush in whatever decision he makes. Why? Because that is what my son would do. Without a doubt, he would serve his commander-in-chief to the best of his ability. I can do no less. God bless all of our sons and daughters who serve.

Dan Kimmett

Thursday, December 12, 2002 1:43 PM

Frank, thank you for your letter. It made me cry. My son was such a great guy. I only wish you could have known him. I am a detective with the Denver Police Department. When my son died I felt like everyone in this country should know of his sacrifice but believed that no one really knew or cared. . . .

He was only 28 but he made a difference in so many lives. He did not have any children but his wife is going through so much. Did you know that when a soldier dies his/her survivors get six months of benefits and then everything ends? My son had insurance but one of the companies refused to pay, citing the Soldier and Sailors Act. His wife now has to struggle with his death and finding a job all at once. . . . Know also that your son, as all who serve, is in my family's prayers. I hope that he returns home safely.

Yours truly,

Dan Kimmett

4

Has John volunteered for this mission because he wants to be a "real Marine," not just the oddball Marine who wrote a book with his dad and got a little bit famous for fifteen minutes? The book was my idea. Have I killed my son?

One of our oldest friends in Boston has a son doing graduate studies at Columbia University. She makes no secret of the fact that she is proud of him for being a leader in the antiwar movement on campus. As young children, John and this kind and intelligent boy played together on family holidays, like Thanksgiving, when our tribes mingled. It's strange in the present circumstances to have John's friend's mother tell me that her son is so "disgusted by this country" that he's traveling to Belgium (where he was born to an American father and his Belgian-American mother), to see if he can "renounce his American citizenship and become Belgian."

When I told John about the fact that his old friend was trying to renounce his citizenship in protest against the war in Afghanistan and the looming war in Iraq, John's reply surprised me. "So?" he said with a smile. "The ones I can't stand are all those college students who don't seem to give a damn."

Peter Mamakos, a member of our church and a former Marine, and a Korean War vet, told John before he left for boot camp, "Just don't volunteer for anything. Do your job but don't go looking for trouble." I wish John had listened to him. John can't tell me where he's going. It's not hard to guess. And I think that he is going to someplace where his six-four frame will be a walking target.

Then I remember that Osama bin Laden is tall! So maybe there are tall Arabs! Will John be mistaken for Osama and shot in a friendly-fire incident? So much for rational thought. . . . The fight for me will be to not tumble into a world of paranoid fantasy. . . . I feel as if I'm losing my marbles.

The unthinkable: My youngest son, my friend, my fishing partner, the sweet freckled kid I've gone to innumerable movies with, the boy who'd won all those eighth-grade basketball games for the IC Pelicans, while I cheered insanely from the bleachers, my little boy I patted to sleep, who got scared when the radiators creaked in the night and who crawled into our bed, my dreamy poet-son who stayed up reading instead of doing homework, might be going to war.

Genie wrote a note.

When friends and acquaintances know you have someone in the military, you can count on a variety of responses. Sometimes I sense a reluctance to even mention John. I've found it best to bring John up first. Depending on their response, I'll decide to elaborate or not. Otherwise, while I can gloss over a lot in a chatty conversation, John's service is like an elephant in the room. I have to at least mention the elephant is sitting on the table in order to move on to other topics.

A friend's reluctance to talk about John going to war may be out of kindness, a natural hesitation to bring up a painful subject, their antiwar politics; or it may just be due to uncertainty, an unwillingness to reveal possible ignorance. So I try to let people know I'm okay, just worried, and John is fine too. Then our conversation can move on.

I know that for some of our more antimilitary friends their politics makes them look at John's service as if he were serving time in jail, not serving his country. And that is tough to take. And sometimes, to avoid a cold shoulder I leave the elephant alone and just don't mention my son.

But I have the e-mails and letters. I share many with Genie to comfort her. When mothers sign notes to me as "proud mother of a Marine," I understand. I find that I am no longer Frank Schaeffer, writer; I'm Frank Schaeffer, proud parent of Corporal John Schaeffer, USMC. I didn't choose this identity. It chose me.

Thursday, February 13, 2003, 10:38 PM

Twenty-one years ago, on February 9th, my wife and I were blessed with the birth of our second son. A small, frail child delivered nine weeks early and holding on to life by an inner will that somehow overcame his severely underdeveloped lungs. He was moved to another hospital immediately after birth. . . . As my wife was doing her best to come out of an epidural fog, she only remembered having the brief chance to see and kiss his hand as they rushed her little boy by helicopter to Children's Hospital. . . .

Now our little guy is a 6 ft 1 in, 195-lb. First Fast Company Special Forces Corporal in the United States Marine Corps, Anti-Terrorist Division. My wife and I drove to Norfolk, Virginia, last November to watch him and his platoon off as they shipped out to Bahrain on a 6-month tour of duty. It was very hard for me to say good-bye and to stand fast to my son who has made me so proud over the years. . . . But for his mother, it was just not a day that she could bear to keep her chin up. . . .

She would not say good-bye there at the end but waited in the car as his sister and I said ours. Then all of a sudden Billy darted over to the car but did not try to look in and catch his mother's eye. It was eerie as he stood there tall and straight, putting his hand in the car on hers, while assuring her that he would return home safely. And . . . she kissed his hand, for that was all she could bring herself to do. And that was plenty.

Alan D. Ross

Wednesday, December 11, 2002 8:48 PM

For too many people it's easy to look at the men and women in uniform as "other," and for too many people in uniform to look at Democrats, leftists, and people who question the administration's Iraq policy as not just "other," but "enemy." Our sons both crossed that gap and lived in the middle where all Americans can share in duty and responsibility, whatever their beliefs about tax policy, welfare, immigration, affirmative action, or guns.

My wife and I took a tour of the carrier *Independence* my son served on before it was decommissioned, and it was eye-opening to see how patched together, dilapidated, and crowded this massive ship was. . . . The scared wives and husbands left at home when deployments are made, and the young kids whose parents are serving, deserve more than food stamps, crappy quarters, and disdain from the elites. . . .

Best wishes to you and your son.

Dave Roberts

Wednesday, December 11, 2002 5:35 PM

I was driving my wife and two toddlers to the staff party at my college last night and, as we were waiting for the light to change, about 60 antiwar protesters were marching in front of our car, escorted and protected by policemen for whom none

of them showed any respect. . . . As they went by, the protesters were blowing their whistles, screaming, banging their
hands on people's hoods—had they touched my vehicle, they
wouldn't have had hands anymore!—and my two babies in
back started crying, horrified by all the noise and commotion.
. . . I looked out at them, mostly white, of course, mostly there
on their parents' dimes, of course, and I wondered . . . why is
it they don't protest Saddam's treatment of women or minorities?
Why aren't they horrified by Saddam's willingness to gas his own
people? It's a very interesting world I live in—in academia—not
sure how much longer I'll be able to take it. . . .

Charles Evered

Sent care of *The Washington Post:*

Thursday, December 19, 2002 1:13 PM

Dear Sirs,

My name is Gregory Commons. I lost my son this past year
in Afghanistan on March 4, 2002, when he was shot and killed
while attempting to rescue a Navy Seal, Neil Roberts, who had
fallen out of a helicopter. My wife, Linda, and I read an article
in *The Washington Post* regarding Mr. Schaeffer's [son]. My
wife was so touched . . . that she wanted to write Mr. Schaeffer.
. . . Please pass along the attached file. . . .

God Bless You,

Sincerely, Greg Commons

Dear Mr. Schaeffer,

. . .

We lost my stepson, Corporal Matthew Commons, on March
4, 2002. Matt was an Army Airborne Ranger, and he was on the

helicopter that was shot down during an attempt to rescue Navy Seal Neil Roberts. Matt was shot and killed as he came out of the helicopter. Six other soldiers died that day, including two other Airborne Rangers. We are devastated and heartbroken by Matt's death, but we are also incredibly proud of him and the other brave young men who fought so hard against such heavy odds that day. . . .

The last time we saw Matt was the week before Christmas, when he was home on block leave. He was deployed to Afghanistan in January, and we got letters, e-mails, and telephone calls from him. We saw the news on Monday, March 4, about the battle at Takur Gar earlier that day, but we figured that Matt was okay, since we hadn't heard anything otherwise. Unfortunately, about 11:30 p.m., a captain from the Mortuary Affairs Office knocked on our door to tell us that Matt had been "mortally wounded" in a rescue attempt in Afghanistan. . . .

Over the past nine months, we have had the privilege of getting to know many of the men from Matt's unit . . . they are all steadfast in their devotion to each other, and to their job. They follow a simple creed—no one is left behind. That is why they were on the mountain on March 4. They also follow the words of Isaiah, as they apply to their mission: God said, whom shall I send? Who will go for me? And they answer: Here I am, send me. I will go for you.

We are supremely grateful for these Rangers, and for the men and women who went before them, and who will come after them, those who are willing to go for us, to lay down their lives so that we may safely sleep at night. We are humbled by their sacrifice, and pray that we will live our lives in such a way to earn what they have paid for.

There is a saying, that for those who have fought for it, freedom has a flavor the protected will never know. Having lost a beloved son, his mother, father, and I have given the best we have to offer. For us, freedom tastes bittersweet, but it is also strongly laced with gratitude.

Sincerely,

Linda Chapman

Tuesday, September 24, 2002

Dear Frank,

. . .

There's a lot about being President that I do *not* miss. But I *do* miss working with our great military. I respect those who serve. I realize that even today, even after 9/11, there are still those who look down on our men/women who serve. Why do several Ivy League schools still hate the military and, yes, the CIA too? There's a cultural arrogance, and your book seems to capture that well.

Thank God for John and the other Marines like him. . . .

All the best,

George Bush

P.S. Your son is "the best you have to offer." Mine is too! GB

Saturday, January 4, 2003

Dear Frank,

One of the greatest joys of the presidency for me was commanding young women and men like your son from many races, religions and backgrounds. Our country is in good hands as long as it has people like John . . .

Sincerely,

Bill Clinton

February 18, 2003 [continued]

I have tapped into a love I've never known. This love isn't about self-interest. It is about something as indispensable as mother's milk: the tie that binds those who serve and those who love them. I have undeservedly stumbled into the America that gives back more than it takes. The sons and daughters of my new "family" are led by officers earning much less than construction workers and commanded by generals making no more than nine times the pay of the lowest-ranking enlisted private.

———————————

[These days our nation's elite and our political leaders who send our sons and daughters to war do not send their own children. It was not always this way.

As eloquently noted by Jon Meacham in his wonderful book, "Franklin And Winston," during the Second World War President Roosevelt and nearly all his top advisors had loved ones serving. Eleanor Roosevelt recalled:

I think my husband would have been very much upset if the boys had not wanted to go into the war immediately, but he did not have to worry very much because they either were already in before the war began, or they went in immediately. . . . Actually we had one advantage, I suppose, and that was that we always did know what was happening in the war picture, and therefore we knew more quickly where our own children were involved, and what was going on, but I think this made us more conscious of the difficulties of parents, whose children were scattered all over, and who couldn't know as quickly as we could—perhaps had weeks of anxiety before they got news of any kind.

The Roosevelt sons James, Elliot, John, and Franklin Jr. all saw action. Robert and Stephen Hopkins, the sons of Roosevelt's most influential advisor and confidant, Harry Hopkins, saw action and Stephen was killed in the Pacific at age 18. Eleanor recalled:

Seeing their sons go off to war was hard on both my husband and Harry Hopkins. Both of them would have liked to take their sons' places . . . I imagine every mother felt as I did when I said goodbye to the children during the war. I had a feeling that I might be saying good-bye for the last time. It was a sort of precursor of what it would be like if your children were killed never to come back. Life had to go on and you had to do what was required of you, but something inside of you died—FS]

What matters in my new universe? Shared memories matter. Genie matters. John matters. Francis matters. Jessica matters, as do her children, Benjamin [seven] and Amanda [ten], and her husband, Dani. And the people in uniform matter and so do their families. What does *not* matter anymore is the sound and fury of our entertainment-addicted celebrity culture that, as a movie director and novelist, I've worked so hard to succeed in.

Wednesday, November 27, 2002 2:41 PM
I am the Deputy General Counsel for the Paralyzed Veterans of America. . . . I am a former Marine corporal (1976–1979). . . . The lack of participation in our armed forces by the more privileged classes . . . is becoming more and more of a problem as less and less legislators have a service background. . . .
William S. Mailander

Thursday, November 28, 2002 11:13 PM

My son graduated high school June 2, 2002, and left for boot camp June 4, 2002. . . . My sister is a 1st Sgt. and has been training female recruits on Parris Island for the last 8 years. . . . It sickens me to know what these men and women are being paid while they make the sacrifices they make for their country (and me.) . . . A college education cannot teach what the USMC can about honor, commitment, discipline, and integrity.

Thank you,

Barbara Dorr

Friday, February 14, 2003 7:53 AM

Subject: Live from Kuwait

Hello, I'm in Kuwait and doing well. I haven't seen Peter yet, but I'm fairly certain I will sometime. Things are being set up and every day this place looks different. We've got a chow hall and tents and all that so I'm not living too rough. I'll probably get to e-mail later, but Peter's at a place with no communication. We're moving soon to an area with little communications but I might at times get a chance to e-mail.

Love you all!

Jane Vizzi Blair

John is in good company. Lieutenant Jane Vizzi Blair is already deployed to Kuwait. I take comfort from knowing that there are officers of her caliber somewhere in my son's chain of command.

[Jane is a friend who enlisted when she was twenty-six and went to boot camp a few months after John did. Before joining the Marines, Jane graduated from Hunter College after studying philosophy and dance. She worked as a human resources associate at JP Morgan.

Now this brilliant, petite, and beautiful woman with fierce blue eyes was a Marine first lieutenant deployed to Kuwait as an air intelligence officer with the 1st Unmanned Aerial Vehicle Squadron serving in Operation Iraqi Freedom and part of the 1st Marine Expeditionary Force. Jane married Marine lieutenant Peter Blair just three days before they were deployed. Peter was also with the 1st Marine Expeditionary Force, as an artillery officer, though sent to another part of the vast operation in the desert, far from Jane. When Jane called to say good-bye, she joked, "Our honeymoon will have to wait."—FS]

Jane e-mails us and calls at odd hours. It's always a relief to hear from her, to recharge our flagging spirits by plugging into her kick-ass cheer.

Sunday, February 16, 2003 2:55 AM
Subject: Kuwait
    Hello! . . . We're moving up to where Peter is near on Tuesday or Wednesday, but I still don't know if I'll see him. We're probably getting an "embedded" reporter and I may have a special TV feature on me, given that I'm a female so "interesting" to the press, because I'm forward deployed into a potential combat area. So keep a look out! I probably won't have e-mail access when I move out.
    The weather is very nice out here but it's a little scary sitting so close to Baghdad . . . however, it's cool that all the news is about us! I heard about the protests—please tell your peace-loving buddies that it's a nice sentiment and all, but they're just keeping us here longer!!! So, tell them to get the hell out of the way and let us do our job!
    Anyway, love you all, and I hope to hear from you soon!
    Jane Vizzi Blair

February 19, 2003

John called this morning at 7:30 AM. I was editing *Zermatt* [my new novel]. Genie was resting, had woken in the night and gone to John's room to sleep on his long, narrow bed below the shelf covered with sports trophies. I didn't know if she woke out of worry for John or from one of her hot flashes. I tiptoed down the stairs and peeked into John's room. Genie's graceful arm was cast up on the pillow above her head. She was breathing gently. The cool dawn filtering through John's window illuminated her ever-young face.

John was on duty all night at his barracks. He had been making his rounds, manning the duty desk and doing whatever it is a Marine corporal "on duty" does. He sounded tired. The barrier of time constraints that sometimes separates us these days was not there. He was so relaxed. For a golden fifteen minutes or so I had my son back, as if it were the old days when he was a kid and everything was simple.

We talked the way we used to when I'd wake him for school then sit on the edge of his bed as he ate a breakfast of hot chocolate and Genie's orange sticky rolls—his favorites—that I'd brought him in an effort to bribe John-the-hater-of-school to get up on a frigid winter morning and plod off to class. Then we'd chat quietly as he munched his way through the mound of rolls, dipping them in his hot chocolate from time to time.

This morning John told me all about the big snowfall that inundated the Washington, D.C., area last night. He described the bulldozers moving the snow, the huge trucks. Then we talked about his training to prepare for his mission.

"I wish I could know what you're doing," I said.

"That's the one downside to this, Dad: I'll never be able to tell you what I did. I don't even know if I'll be allowed to tell you where I am. Maybe I will once I get there."

"That's going to be tough," I said.

"Yeah," John sighed. "You know, a lot of people in the intel deal get divorced. I don't think it's good not being able to talk to your family. You ought to hear the stories I get told, though!" He laughed.

"Like what?"

"See, that's the problem. I can't tell you," John chuckled. "That's probably why they're all divorced."

As we talked I looked at the three two-inch wire figures that perch in a row on my computer monitor. John made them for me out of champagne cork fasteners. For years John has taken the wire from champagne bottles and fashioned it into little figures. His miniature "sculptures" litter the kitchen: running men, a pole-vaulter, various warriors, a swimmer, jumper, sumo wrestler. They perch on photograph frames, atop candlesticks, on the seashells in the big basket of shells we've spent years collecting from our walks on Plum Island beach. Birthday parties, Christmas, Thanksgiving, and every time my agent sold one of my books provided an excuse for cel-ebratory champagne and John with another wire fastener.

The three figures on my computer are a writer holding a quill, a reader with an open book, and a Greek warrior with a round shield. The shield is made from the metal cap that was over the cork on a bottle of Moët & Chandon; the writer's "quill" is a feather from a pillow; and the "book" is a bit of folded paper. These particular fasteners came from John's twenty-second birthday party. He'd been home on leave for a few days. He made them with his beautiful big hands while sitting at the kitchen table, then tossed them over to me with a "Here, these are for you, Pop." The little figures have come to represent my son to me: writer, poet, and warrior.

Late in the afternoon John called back.

"It's official," he said. "I'm definitely going."

"We're proud of you," I said, while trying to keep the panic out of my voice.

"Yes," Genie added, "we are."

After the call, Genie and I went for a long walk down the Plum Island tidal flat. The light on the calm water, sand, and sky melted into a winter vision of shimmering pink sunset. John had splashed his way along that beach on summer afternoons in what now seems to be another lifetime. He ate the sand by the fistful when he was a baby, played war in the dunes as a child, ran races with me and his brother and sister.

I studied the sand as if I hoped to glimpse his footprints from some long-past carefree afternoon, frozen under the thin layer of ice. We've had such a snowy winter, snow on snow! There is a war brewing and the snowplow driver has no place left to put the snow on our drive. It's the deepest it's ever been in the twenty-three years we've owned our home. After this winter—this winter of impending war, anti-American marches all over the world, "orange" and "yellow" terror alerts, of John volunteering to go to war—snow will always remind me of "that awful winter of 2003."

When we got home I needed a slug of antacid before I could have my evening glass (or three) of red wine. It's been years since my stomach acted up. I'm drinking more.

Does Genie blame herself for something? Is she racking her brain, as I am, for clues as to why John's life has turned out this way? Does she think that somehow we could have done something differently, something that would have made him stay closer to a life path that would let us sleep well at night? Would she want that? Would I?

With John about to go to war, Genie and I are nosing our way back along the trail of our lives. We want to figure out what the hell we've done (or not done) to produce this strapping Marine, to get ourselves into this nightmare, one where pride and fear mix in equal blood-pressure-popping proportions. We've got to be the least typical Marine parents in the country. How did we get here? Why is John a Marine? Where did this come from? Looking for answers, Genie wrote:

When John decided to join the Marines, I thought to myself, "John, are you really going to be able to take orders? You certainly never have from me!" But I've learned mothers are in a special category all to themselves!

When John was starting second grade, I decided to home-school him. We were going to be out of the country making a film in South Africa and Namibia, so it seemed like a good time since he'd be absent that academic year.

He'd been happy enough in the regular classroom during his first school years but after a good start he'd begun taking long periods of time spacing out if he found the subject boring. Math was the worst. He wasn't disruptive; he was sitting quietly at his desk, doing nothing. I thought he needed a year to mature a little. I would be able to get him to concentrate better. I'd get a mail-order curriculum and do it myself. I'd coached Jessica and Francis through math and reading problems. I knew I could do it with John.

In retrospect, homeschooling John was a mixed blessing, to say the least. Even though I'd invent games and use objects to illustrate the math calculations, as soon as the fun stuff was over, and I'd ask him to do 10 minutes of a worksheet, just a few problems that we'd gone over together, he would stare at the page of numbers, sweetly, passively spacing out, ignoring me. If he got five problems done with me sitting next to him, it was a good day and we moved on. I tried rewards. I tried punishments. Nothing would motivate him. I would walk away so infuriated.

Fortunately the other parts of the "program" that year worked much better. Writing was fine. Reading was a pleasure, as was ancient history and nature studies. Visiting the local museums, plus the eight months spent in Africa, meant that, all in all, it was a good year.

But I learned a valuable lesson: I could not fill every role in life. As a disciplinarian, I lacked fortitude! I did not have what *it takes. I started feeling mean and/or wimped out. And John knew it. I gained the utmost respect for teachers.*

John grew up to be the most patient, persistent, intelligent, quiet, perceptive, and funny person I've ever known. I kept waiting for him to connect with a subject, discover a passion—some aspect of learning that he would find rewarding enough to pursue for its own sake. But John continued to work (or not) at school in his own fashion; patiently ignoring our exhortations; skipping what did not interest him. He could just be so lazy! This drove us nuts.

Over the years Frank and I had more fights about John and his education than any other issue. It was ridiculous. The cry would go up: "Oh, what will become of this child!" and we were off screaming at each other again.

I think that as far as John was concerned, doing well in school was no great achievement. Though he felt glad for his friends and their academic successes, school just didn't mean much to him.

So when it turned out that the one thing John could see himself going after was the Marines, I was stunned.

"Are you sure?"

"Yes, I want the training and the discipline."

"You do?!"

After urging him all through senior year to "get it together" and figure something out, I couldn't exactly say "no," especially because I knew nothing about the Marines. It was time for me to study and learn some hard lessons that I'd been avoiding. For one thing, I needed to learn about patriotism.

I was also relieved in a strange way. I'd feared the potential disaster of John coasting through college, entering the netherworld of habitual indecision and prolonged adolescence, with minimum adult supervision but maximum financial support. I had always hoped John would follow his big sister and brother's example and pursue a course of study as a preparation for an adult life, with graduation seen as a final rite of passage. For John, it was not to be, at least not right out of high school. The Marines take care of all that "rite of passage" stuff in one year or less! In the Corps it didn't take four years for John to grow up. And while I don't know as much about other Marines, John—with the exception of a year stuck waiting for his security clearance—has been continually challenged, trained, and motivated by the Corps. The Marine Corps has been good for John . . . so far.

5

Even before I was a writer and long before I began the diary that makes up much of this book, for years I felt isolated. I had a strange childhood and an odd series of professions. Genie and I are both "self-unemployed," as we always told the kids when they wanted something we couldn't afford. My children had trouble trying to explain my jobs to their friends.

My "commute" is to walk down the steep stairs from our bedroom in the renovated attic of our 1835 brick house, take a right, and walk five steps to Jessica's old bedroom, complete with her well-worn set of Beatrix Potter books still on the fireplace mantel. I sit at my cluttered desk, open the Word file of the day, and start to write. My view past the computer monitor, upon which John's wire figures now crouch, is of a green-beige field of reeds and marsh grass rippling in the breeze, or flattened and bedraggled under snow. Beyond the marsh are the sluggish gray waters of the Merrimack River flowing in and out with the tides, glistening under a hot sun in summer, and in winter, filled with big flat chunks of ice. Genie has farther to go, all the way to the first floor, down a whole extra flight of narrow back stairs to her office.

Genie runs a small mail-order company consisting of her, a barn full of books, cards, and calendars, and in the afternoons, me as her part-time "packing and shipping department." Our life together is one wherein we live, work, and love as a tightly knit country of two. This existence seems claustrophobic to us on some days, wonderful on others, and idyllic to friends, especially to the ones who never happen to overhear the decibel level of our battles. I once heard Francis tell a friend that "my mom and dad work together, and 'labor disputes' in our house rival those really bitter coal miners' strikes . . . you know, the kind where the National Guard gets called in!"

Genie's childhood was normal enough, if any childhood converging with adolescence in San Francisco in the 1960s can be called "normal." She has two brothers and two sisters. Her father is a lawyer and her mother a homemaker. Genie's youth was part and parcel of the Bay Area hippie drug culture, soundtrack courtesy of the Jefferson Airplane, Grateful Dead, et al. But Genie can explain her childhood to our friends. My childhood is a different matter. And no one, least of all me, can believe that I've produced a Marine.

I was raised by American fundamentalist Presbyterian missionary parents in Switzerland. My dad never served. At age eleven I was packed off to a British boarding school after my parents woke up to the fact that my "homeschooling"—my older sisters took erratic turns teaching me, while I stared out the window at the Alps—hadn't worked too well. In other words, I could hardly read.

After graduating from a wonderful all-boys English primary and middle school, what the English call a "prep school," I was sent to another boys' boarding school, in Wales—a horror of a private high school, what the English refer to as a "public school," as harsh as the austere rocky coast it clung to. I ran away from this bleak fortress when I was fifteen. (Lindsay Anderson's movie *If.* . . . still gives me grim satisfaction!)

After skulking back to Switzerland, much to my parent's consternation, I did what the contemporary gurus of peace and love advocated: dropped out and turned on. I painted large German expressionist-style canvases, smoked a little pot, drank a lot of wine, and partied with the mostly American and English young people who came to the mission. I chased the girls and shot Super-8 mm movies. I got a job doing the light show at a big raunchy discothéque in Montreux—more consternation from my long-suffering parents! Then I met Genie.

Along with her older sister Pam, Genie had taken the old yellow postal bus from the valley up to the mission to visit a friend. The first night of their visit I lured Genie—the most beautiful girl I had ever seen—into my basement painting-studio/pad with a promise that she could listen to the just-released Beatles album *Abbey Road*.

About six months after we met, I got Genie pregnant and we fell in love, but not in that order. I was seventeen and she was eighteen. We married on June 20, 1970, just as Genie—wearing a crown of daisies—was beginning to "show," a Renaissance princess stepping from a portrait by Botticelli. We had Jessica, then Francis, and conceived a third child—Corporal John Schaeffer, USMC—just before we moved to America in 1980, where he was born in Haverhill, Massachusetts. As the third child John got a father who was more relaxed than I'd been with my first two children. I was actually beginning to acquire some parental skills. As a result I was less up-tight about everything with John, and we became close as two peas in a pod.

Genie and I bought our old wreck of a house and fixed it up a room at a time, with the kids helping. I stopped painting and directed documentaries, some commercials, and four feature films, none good, the last being *Baby on Board* for ABC, starring Judge Reinhold and Carol Kane. I quit the movie business with a sigh of relief when, in 1992, my first novel was published to good reviews. I began to write full time, feeling fortunate that I had discovered my calling.

None of our a-rolling-stone-gathers-no-moss experiences gave Genie and me a common bond with any community until 1990, when we joined the local Greek Orthodox Church. Then, in 1999, John joined the Marines.

Church connected us to new friends, warm embraces from short, mothering Greek ladies, and a glorious liturgical tradition. John's service connected us to heroes. Some have watery eyes and blue-veined hands. Some marched into the abyss as boys and were reborn as men in dark places like Iwo Jima, Guadalcanal, and, in one case, a Japanese prisoner of war camp. I had hardly noticed they were my neighbors, before John joined. After John became a Marine, I discovered they had been all around me.

While, in some cases, over half a century separated my son and the heroes of past wars, they were his brothers, and therefore family to Genie and me. John being in the Corps also bound us to mothers in trailer parks with children riding on their hips, and to their young husbands in sweltering, fly-swarmed tents waiting for the ultimate command, and to thousands of forlorn, scared parents just like us, waiting for news of sons and daughters.

February 20, 2003

Genie has become absentminded since the news of John's pending deployment. She's often silent. I have to repeat myself sometimes. Her mind is with John. They were so beautiful together, the young mother sitting with her little child, both staring into my camera lens one Christmas morning. I stop writing and reach out to touch the picture of them.

Genie and I talk about John and how Jessica has not seen him for so long, how disappointed she'll be when we tell her that he'll be deployed when she comes to visit this spring. We know Francis will be sad too. He's often spoken of how much he's looking forward to being with his brother and sister, all in the same place at the same time again for the first time in four years.

I've been looking forward to Jessica's visit and seeing my grand-children. Will I screw it up? Will I brood, resenting whatever good times we're having because John is in harm's way?

"How do you feel about this?" I asked John after he called to say it was official.

"Nervous," answered John.

"Will you have to start any other special training?" I asked.

"It depends where I'll be going."

"I mean, when will you decide to?" I asked.

"Dad, I don't 'decide,'" answered John, sounding slightly annoyed.

"Oh, you mean you're a Marine or something? You mean it's not up to you?" I asked, and laughed as best I could.

Tonight I'm jealous of John's friends who aren't serving and of their parents' peace of mind. I'm also wondering about John's girlfriend Mollie, how she'll take his deployment.

Francis called. He is being so kind. [I admire Francis's love of his teaching vocation. After being awarded the highest academic honor given by the School of Foreign Service at Georgetown University, he had numerous graduate studies offers but chose to teach at his old high school, a job he loves.—FS]

Francis is a "natural" teacher. I know because when he tried to teach me to use a computer I was his worst student ever, a cranky dyslexic. During the six months he lived at home [after graduating in 1997, and before getting his own apartment], Francis overcame my can't-teach-an-old-dog-new-tricks, never-fixed-my-childhood-dyslexia-so-don't-even-*try* stubbornness. . . .

"*It's ALL disappeared!*" I bellowed.

"Dad, it's three in the morning," Francis said sleepily as I turned on his light.

"But I'm *writing*, or was trying to until *you* ruined it all! Damn machine! It took it away!"

Francis slipped on his bathrobe and followed me to my office.

"No, Dad, don't worry, you just minimized the file by mistake. See? You click there and it all comes back!"

"Are you telling me that this damned thing can just send my manuscript away?"

"Dad, it's not sending it away; just, when you click on that little box it minimizes it."

"Well, tell it to stop that! How can you write a novel if some machine gets to 'minimize' it? What the hell? Oh, *how* I wish Genie would just type up everything the way she used to!"

"But Dad, you yelled at her too much," said Francis with a smile.

"I did not! *Why would I do that?*" I yelled.

"For the same reason you're yelling at me. You just aren't very patient. Now see, look what you can do with this nifty little spell-check. It'll fix all those words with the red lines under them. . . ."

Francis never shouted back. He would have made a great psychiatrist.

6

Genie wrote me this note. I found it tucked into my briefcase while on the plane. I had asked her how she was doing. This is her answer.

Now we know that John is going, most nights I don't sleep well; I have a sense of continual unease. Some days it is hard to get my bearings so I try to keep life simple. I notice I've begun to resent things that feel too frivolous or a waste of time.

Church and prayer give me comfort. The recitation of the liturgy and psalms are particularly good. The continuity of the holy days and the community life centered on the sacraments tide me over during the times I can't sense God's grace.

Frank, you are wonderful to me. We discuss how John's absence feels and you know how to describe the void. You get on with your writing and our lives. You recognize what needs to happen and do it. You're not afraid to correct yourself. You are wild and funny at the most unexpected moments, a force of nature, the love of my life and I'm glad I have you. I could not get through this without you.

I am in awe of military families. The strength and determination required to hold up through all the uncertainties that come with the military life is enormous. And there are families that do this for generations! I couldn't admire them more. I'm trying to learn to be as strong.

My parents have a quiet strength that I have always taken for granted. I now know their stoicism comes from having a parent or other close family members die young, growing up in the Depression, getting married while both were serving in the military during WWII. I understood none of this growing up. Now, with John going to war, I am starting to understand why my parents are so strong and what made them that way.

I had a reading and book signing at Barnes & Noble tonight. It was the first reading from our book I've done since hearing John will be deployed.

There was a young Air Force staff sergeant at the reading. This morning some peace demonstrators outside a local college he was driving past pounded on his car. He had his uniform on and they surrounded his car and screamed and spit at him when he stopped for the light. He was still shaken.

Before the reading, the Air Force sergeant's friend, a local acquaintance of mine, took me aside and told me how upset his buddy was. "He wasn't scared of those guys," said his friend. "It was just a big shock to know that he was so hated by the people he'll be trying to defend." The sergeant is leaving tomorrow and had to give his terrier to his mother to care for while he is gone. That was where he had just come from when the demonstrators pounded on his car. He had wanted to wear his dress uniform, "to make his mom proud," said his friend. The sergeant is only twenty-three. He ships out to the Gulf tomorrow. He looks much younger than his age.

At the back of the near-empty bookstore I read John's account of his life in boot camp to my small audience. I had trouble keeping my voice steady as I read his words. Later I made a big point of shaking the sergeant's hand and thanking him for his service. I wanted to be formal about it. But his short haircut reminded me of John, and before I stopped to think I hugged him.

Saturday, February 22, 2003 4:56 PM

Four years in the Marine Corps were the most memorable years of my life. During Desert Storm and Somalia I was proud to be America's best on the front lines. . . . It's strange how parents feel they have it all figured out for their kids as they get older and churn out cookie cutter young adults into American life. Parents always have this plan laid out for their kids. "Go to school, graduate college, start a career, buy a house, get married and have kids." It's good to hear that kids like John want to break away from this mold and seek out more in life to have a true sense of honor and meaning. . . .

"Some people spend an entire lifetime wondering if they've made a difference. The Marines don't have that problem."

—President Ronald Reagan

Semper Fi,
Jorge Silva

Saturday, February 22, 2003 10:42 PM

I am a member of the Oklahoma Air National Guard. . . . On the morning of 9/11, I had worked the midnight shift. I worked "mids" because . . . I could watch our kids during the day and keep them out of day care as my wife went to work.

I watched the footage from the first tower strike. I have, unfortunately, worked military aircraft crash sites, and knew by looking at the damage a civilian airliner was involved. My first thought was: Who violated the FAA bubble around the towers? I was on the phone with my Air National Guard Unit when the second tower was struck.

After a short pause I stated, "Guess we know this was intentional; better start a recall and get on locking down the base."

Many of the other guard members showed up to our unit, ready to go to work without a call. These people left home, work, and their families and reported. The slang is "running to the sound of gunfire." Since this day, all of our troops have gone overseas, many of them on their third rotation. . . . As I write to you I am waiting on an airlift to take me overseas.

I am also the "black sheep" of my family. My mother is a physician, father a CPA, one brother a businessman and one a teacher. I am a police officer and a member of the armed services, and proud to be. . . .

Stay the course.
Sincerely
Robert Baird, Cap 138 SFS/CC
Oklahoma Air National Guard

3:30 AM. My father and John were together. Dad wanted to give John a Bible study. John did not have his Bible. "Go back to your room and get your Bible," my father said to John. "I want to hear you read out loud." John went upstairs. Dad and I were left sitting in a strange and beautiful garden. Then Dad faded away. I was waiting for John to come back and longing to talk to my Dad, to tell him what was gnawing at my guts, making me feel so homesick.

I woke up in this sterile little motel room with tears on my cheeks. I don't know if I was crying for Dad or John. I miss my dad tonight. He's been dead almost twenty years. He would have been proud of his grandson. I know. Dad always spoke with such pride about his father's Spanish-American War service in the U.S. Navy.

February 24, 2003. Back Home

10:20 PM. John just called. He's been issued his gear. He has all new cammies, sand-colored for desert. He has mountain boots and desert boots and, most chilling to me, a bulletproof vest to wear under civilian clothes, as well as a flak jacket if he's deployed in uniform. What the hell will he be doing?

I could tell John was thrilled and yet he was trying mightily to keep his voice subdued for my sake. He could sense my worry and kept trying to sound sober and grown up. But I could hear in his voice that he really wanted to shout: "ISN'T THIS ALL *SO* COOL?!"

"Wear your bulletproof vest," I said somewhat grumpily.

John laughed.

"I will when I need to."

"Do me a favor and wear it for us even when you feel safe."

"Okay, sure, but it's only good for a kill shot—I mean it only covers my spine, heart, and lungs."

"That's a start. So wear it."

"Yeah, right, Dad."

"What else did they give you?"

"A new Kevlar [helmet], a seabag, three flight bags, two packs."

"How did you get all that back to your barracks?"

"Shopping carts . . . loaded up, then got them to the vehicle."

"Well, when you go, I want to know everything you can tell me . . . I mean, that you're allowed to tell."

"Well, I won't know what I'm allowed to say till later."

"But when you do, tell us where you are."

"Sure, but I may not know for a while," John said.

There was a pause. John's excited calmness—for lack of a better description—was pissing me off, and at the same time making me proud of him. I wanted to dive through the phone and grab my son by the arm and drag him home, or at least give him a good shaking and yell: "This isn't a game! You're killing us!"

"So when do you think you'll be going?" I asked.

"There's about eight weeks special training, then we'll be sent."

"What if the war with Iraq starts?"

"Then it may get crunched a little. I don't know."

"When does training start for the mission?"

"Wednesday." John paused. He must have picked up the hollow sound in my voice, because the next thing he said was, "You'll feel a lot more confident I'll be okay when you see all this equipment. They've really got everything here!"

Nothing scares me more than his youthful bravado.

"Good. What about your weapons?" I asked somberly.

"I won't be keeping those here, but I'll be out on the range training."

"With a sidearm?"

"Yes, a 9 millimeter and the M-16, and the M-4 too. The M-4 is different. Shorter barrel, shorter stock, better in constricted conditions."

"Will you train with the weapons you take with you?"

"No. We'll be issued those before we go."

"But they'll let you sight them in, right?"

"Dad!" said John, sounding as exasperated as he used to when I'd bug him one time too many about making sure he'd remembered to bring his shin guards for soccer. "They *know* how to do this! Of *course* we'll be able to sight in our weapons!"

"Good, because I was just thinking that you'd want to practice with the actual weapon you'll have and—"

Now definitely exasperated: "This is *all* they do, Dad! They *KNOW* how to do it!"

"Right, right," I said hastily.

7

It is snowing hard. I sit at the base visitor center waiting for John for an hour. When he strides in he is wearing his cammies. We hug, then walk over to the desk to get my visitor pass.

"I have some news for you," John says. "But I'll wait till later to tell you."

The security officer filling in the information on my pass pipes up. "Is it news of deployment?"

"Maybe," growls John.

We step out into the snow.

"It looks like I could be sent over there in two weeks, not six," says John.

———

With all that is going on in Iraq, I knew something like this might happen. I'm feeling ill, empty, trying to be cheerful for John's sake.

John's room in the barracks is strewn with all his new gear. When I ask him to John models his bulletproof vest and a desert sun hat and cammie jacket. The bulletproof vest looks so small on him! It leaves so much exposed! I take pictures. I have only five shots left on the roll. As the camera rewinds I think back to all the many hundreds of photographs I've shot of my son. I have to push away melodramatic thoughts.

When we go to dinner, John is distracted. He talks and jokes and, for a bit, is his old self—not his most relaxed self, but relaxed enough to eat and kid around. He will have to pack six weeks of training into two. From eight weeks to six to two! He is acting like a cat that has just spotted a dog—edgy.

After dinner, John keeps checking off items on a to-do list. Everything is written down in a little green book: equipment he needs, shots he must get, like vaccinations and TB tests.

"It will be interesting," John says.

"Not too 'interesting,' I hope," I grumble.

"Well, more interesting than you'll like," John answers with a grin. "But no need to tell Mom that."

John goes outside to smoke his bedtime cigarette. He gave up smoking until a few weeks ago. Now he's started again.

February 27, 2003. Ronald Reagan Airport

A snowstorm is threatening on the CNN map. I'm hoping the snow doesn't screw up Genie's visit. I'm on my way home. She's flying down tomorrow to say good-bye to John while I head to California to do a book signing.

I say my "good-byes" to John several times this morning. Before I went to sleep last night he was rereading P. J. O'Rourke's *Holidays in Hell* and chuckling quietly. I kept surreptitiously raising my head to watch him. I didn't want to sleep while I still had the chance to see my son. I woke up in the dark a little before he did and listened to him breathing.

When John wakes up I borrow his prayer book and sit on the edge of his bed. As I make the sign of the cross over his chest I cannot help but think of that small bulletproof vest, pray that he'll wear it, pray that if he gets shot the bullet will hit the plate.

The words of the ancient Greek Orthodox prayers comfort me.

I hold my son's hand as we pray. At first his grip is tight; I think John is remembering all he has to do that day. But as we pray his hand relaxes. . . .

Lord, I have cried unto Thee, hear me. Hear me, O Lord.
Lord, I have cried unto Thee, hear me. Receive the voice of
my supplication when I cry to Thee. Hear me, O Lord. Let
my prayer be set forth as incense before Thee. . . .

We are standing in a snowy parking lot opposite the base. John is in his cammies, wearing his cammie cover. I shake his hand, then kiss him good-bye.

"God bless you, John. Come home safe," I say.

"I'll work on it," John answers.

"I love you, John. I'm proud of you."

"I love you, too, Dad."

John walks away.

I call after him, "I love you, son!"

John turns and kisses the air. I get back in the rented car but don't drive until he is out of sight and I can get the tears out of my eyes.

Lord, I have cried unto Thee. . . .

February 28, 2003

I'm on the plane to California. Genie dropped me off at the airport this morning. This afternoon she will try, snowstorm notwithstanding, to fly down to see John for the weekend and say good-bye. He could go any day now, they say.

As we parted I told Genie that I believe God will protect John. She looked so beautiful with the tears welling in her eyes, so vulnerable. She can still break my heart with a look.

"Maybe I'll feel better once I see him," said Genie.

"Yes, you will," I answered. "All those Marines are running around trying to get sent out on these task force intel missions. You'll meet some great guys who have gone out and come back safe and sound."

I held her hand. It was trembling.

We are both tired and spread thin. I'm coming down with the flu. I want to lash out at everyone who has anything to do with the world situation right now, anyone who is part of the events that are putting my son at risk. I know that I'm in a mood to make a fool of myself.

8

To love a child going to a war is to admit that the mystery of sacrifice is greater than any explanation of it. To come to rely on my e-mail correspondents, who have reached out because of the brotherhood their sons and daughters share with my son, is undeserved grace. I'm learning again, as I did with the birth of each of my children, that the most deeply meaningful events in my life are those I can't control: undeserved love, love without safe limits, love that is founded on a sacrifice made by another.

In the case of John's birth the sacrifice was Genie's. He got stuck. He was a big baby—twenty-three inches long, and he weighed in at ten pounds three ounces. Genie was in labor for thirty-six hours and John had to be tugged from her with forceps to the sound of her long cry.

Holding John after he was born, watching him crawl through the sun-warmed tidal pools on Plum Island and, later, at weekly soccer matches, his blond hair backlit and fiery from the late afternoon sun, his lanky body racing up the sideline to stop the attacking team, I'd forget my ambitions and simply *be*. . . .

I sent out an e-mail to my military "family" to say that John is being deployed. I went online an hour later and wondered if there was some problem with my computer; my in-box was jammed. There was a torrent of messages of support, prayers, friendship, and good advice.

Wednesday, March 05, 2003 2:35 PM
Wish your son luck . . . I'll be finding out in about 2 weeks if my reserve unit gets activated. Before your son leaves, make him a little survival kit.

Toilet paper (This is like gold out there and they are going through a shortage)
Eye drops (The sand is very fine and irritates the eyes)
Saline nasal spray (Many bloody noses occur because of the sand)
Sunblock
Chapstick with sun block
Baby powder
Baby wipes (Without the powder and wipes, many understand what a baby goes through when they have diaper rash!)
Q-tips
Scarves or some type of protective mask (You sit through a few sandstorms and you'll wish you had something to cover your face)
Form-fitting leather gloves
Sunglasses (1 nice pair and about 4 cheap pairs)
Goggles (Units are supposed to issue these but many have had a shortage of supplies)
Disposable camera (You send him cameras and he can send them back for you to develop)

History is in the making. . . .

Semper Fi,
Jorge Silva
SGT, USMC

Wednesday, March 05, 2003 4:44 PM
We have John in our prayers. My son Scott was deployed to Kuwait on January 20th. Not much news from him lately. Mail is Oh So Slow. . . . There are too many soldiers using too few phones and computers. . . . We sent a care package to him four weeks ago and he hasn't received it yet. If you can get an early APO address for John once he's deployed, you'll be way ahead in getting mail to him. . . .
Timothy E. Sawyers

Wednesday, March 05, 2003 6:21 PM
Placing John's name near the Sacrament on the altar for his protection by the side of the Prince of Peace, He knows what He is doing, long term.
+Fr. Roger Fleurant

Wednesday, March 05, 2003 9:27 PM
I never worried when I was being deployed. However, now that it might be our sons, I'm very concerned. I'm not worried about the performance of our sons. I believe they will make us proud. I just don't know what to expect. . . . When I left for Desert Storm I can still picture my wife standing in the door with tears coming down her face. . . . I'm starting to understand her feelings with my sons involved. . . .
Ed Michael

March 6, 2003

John called and, sounding somewhat disappointed, said, "They say that I could get sent anytime but it won't be as soon as they thought."

John's deployment has been postponed by anywhere from a few days to a month!

"When will you know?" I asked.

"Not till they say. I don't know anything. I'm just supposed to stay ready."

I'm not sure how to react. It is a strange situation. We have said our good-byes and he is still here. I want to go down and be with him, but what would we do? I can't just sit and stare at him. This new twist is ratcheting up the tension. I want him here, yet if he's going I just want to get this over with.

I get word that the segment on ABC's *20/20* about our book will run this Friday. Then the producer calls back to say our show segment has been postponed. It's ironic—none of my books have ever gotten this sort of attention before, but I don't give a damn about the promotion at this point. It's impossible to concentrate on anything but my anxiety for John.

I called John to let him know that *20/20* is postponed. He didn't care. In fact, he barely listened to me.

"How is it all going?" I asked.

"Fine."

"So you don't know when you're going yet?"

"Dad, don't ask me every day. I'll tell you as soon as I have any real information."

"I'm not asking you 'every day.' I've only talked to you twice this week."

"Then don't ask every time you call."

I long to have some sort of heart-to-heart with John, but neither Genie nor I can pour out our fears to him. This is so odd. I think my job is to keep everything reassuringly normal, though I don't know what "normal" is these days. In fact, I have no idea how to get through this.

I carry an ache under my solar plexus. John does not want me badgering him. Now that he may be here for another week or two, I'm looking for any excuse to find something to do for my son so I can see him again before he goes.

———————

So, damn it, I'm buying a new car to replace the old Ford Taurus! I've been needing to do this for a while anyway. Then I'll drive the old one to John, if it makes it down there—it only has 183,000 miles on it. Then, for the remaining days or weeks before he ships out, he'll have wheels! When he comes back he'll have a car.

———————

"You are?" asked Genie.

"I want to see him and this seems right."

Genie looked at me with her okay-but-I-don't-quite-get-this look.

Later, John took my nutty gesture in stride.

"Okay, Dad, if you want to, but I don't really need a car right now. I mean, I'm leaving."

"I want you to have it!"

"Sure, right. Thanks."

9

I stomp up my snowy driveway in the dark to collect my copy of the *Times*. The first sliver of gray cracks the horizon. "We're a nuclear power," I mutter darkly as I stomp back to the house in the dark. "We send young Marines armed with M-16s to fight an enemy that hides in rat holes like Pakistan and Saudi Arabia that we won't go after. . . . They're a bigger threat than that old blowhard Saddam. . . . The President says the Saudis are our 'friends'! . . . The *Times* says we must show 'restraint'! Let the publisher show restraint with *his* son! Why aren't the *President's* daughters serving—then he'd nuke Mecca!"

I marched into the kitchen fuming.

"Talking to yourself?" asked Genie, who was padding around in her bathrobe and fixing coffee.

"No!"

"About what?"

"The fact that the President and the publisher of the *Times* have no skin in the game! That's *'what'*!"

"It's a little early, don't you think?"

"Happy fanatics! Sure, seventy dark-eyed virgins are waiting for them . . . planning to kill our son!"

"Right now he's sitting at his base. Let's take it a day at a time."

After liturgy, Byron hugged me. Byron Matthews is one of three former Marines in our congregation. He is tall, thin, and stands straight as a mast. The hug was awkward. My face was briefly pressed against his lapel, and the sharp edge of the little American flag pin he's been wearing since 9/11 poked my cheek.

"How's John?" Byron asked gruffly.

"He's being sent over any day now," I said.

Byron's eyes filled with tears. He looked away.

"He'll be fine," Byron growled. He had to pause before adding, "He's a good kid."

"I know," I said miserably.

Byron never tears up. He had never hugged me. He is a strong and distinguished man and was responsible for the restoration of historic downtown Newburyport during the years he was mayor. His hug, teary eyes, and brusque manner said more than anything else could.

March 10, 2003

John called tonight; he sounded excited. He had been on the range firing an M-16 and learning to use the 9 millimeter.

"You just point the pistol and shoot," he said happily. "As for the M-16, of course, all I did was take ten shots to sight in, and then I qualified. It was easy, nothing like the Marine qual back on Parris Island, too easy."

My spirits rose. It's hard to be sad when John sounds so jazzed.

Genie transferred the ownership of our old car today. Tomorrow I'll drive it to him.

10

I rant to my old friend Frank Gruber in a way I can't to anyone else. Frank is an entertainment lawyer and local columnist living in Santa Monica, California. We've been close friends for more than fifteen years and have written some scripts together.

Frank is a secular Jew and I'm a practicing Orthodox Christian. He's a self-described man of the "left." I'm all over the map ideologically, but more conservative than Frank. I'm married to Genie, a woman who publishes books on theology and who bore her children when she was very young. Frank is married to Janet, a wonderful friend, a great hostess, and an atheist philosophy professor of the far left who waited to have a child till she was forty. I tend to be pessimistic about the state of the world. Frank is an optimist who believes in progress and the goodness of just about everybody but Republicans. My son joined the Marines. Frank is cozily embedded, along with Janet and his delightful teenage son, Henry, in a wealthy community known as the "People's Republic of Santa Monica," a place that probably produces fewer Marines per square mile than any town in America.

Frank and I argue over the phone and via e-mail almost daily. I love Frank like a brother and, like a real family member, tend to be incredibly rude to him. And Frank's concern and friendship helped me get through many a tough day as John went to war.

From: Frank Schaeffer
Monday, March 10, 2003 8:40 PM
To: Frank Gruber
Dear Frank:

I'm pissed off with everyone! I blame the fundamentalists, all of you! Fundamentalists (religious, secular, of the left and right and all points in between) dream of making their ideas dominant and wind up getting young men like my son sent to war. Fundamentalists of every persuasion believe that if their crusades succeed they will "improve" the human race. I don't want to be improved! (And if you're not a fundamentalist, albeit of the secular left, then why do you care so much about winning the culture wars? You say you don't believe in moral absolutes but you believe that absolutely!)

I blame the fundamentalists of American exceptionalism and their neoconservative shills who proclaim "a better world" is just around the corner if only we force democracy on everyone. Where are their sons and daughters tonight? Not in the military, I bet!

What are we doing in the Middle East? I'm furious with the West Bank settlers in Israel! Their silly Zionist messianic delusions have stirred up a hornet's nest! And last, but not least, what's not to loathe about the Saudis and their unrelenting export of hate-filled Islamic extremism? I'm irate with you liberals too! Your idea of diplomacy is vacillation and appeasement! What's your answer for naked aggression, torture, and oppression? "Multicultural diversity"? "Multilateral talks"?

We humans exist someplace between worse and not so bad. There are no utopias. No "Big Ideas," Islamic, Christian, Jewish, socialist, or otherwise will solve all our problems. Your trust in "progressive" causes "liberating" mankind is nonsense. My son and his brother Marines settle for keeping things from getting worse on their watch. John won't make a "better world" but is honorably doing his part to keep us a little safer for a little while. He is doing his part to push back the night of chaos on his watch. That is a lot, and all any generation can do. It is the way civilization always defends itself. There are no permanent solutions to chaos and evil, just ceaseless vigilance.

John's departure got postponed; so now I'm driving down to say good-bye all over again.

Best,

Frank

From: Frank Gruber
Monday, March 10, 2003 9:08 PM
To: Frank Schaeffer
Subject: Your latest diatribe

Frank,

In case we don't talk tonight, I suggest you take a couple of deep breaths, give John the best love and regards from us you can give him at a distance and in proxy. I'd say we were all praying for him, but you'd know my verb would be wrong. But we think about him a lot.

Love to you and Genie, too.

Frank

March 11, 2003

It's all very well for Frank to say take a deep breath. I am *not* calm! I turned on the TV and there are high school children skipping classes to protest the war. When asked by the reporter why he was marching, one of them turned to the camera and answered, "War is like, dumb." I wonder if the adult organizers who set up this march ever told these tongue-pierced infants that if it had not been for another "dumb war" every Jew, gypsy, homosexual, and Slav in Europe would have been gassed. I wonder if they told these kids that the African-American student next to them is free because other children's fathers went to war and died by the tens of thousands.

I drive our old car to John. He is waiting at the base visitor center. This is our second farewell.

"I have news. I'm going next week," John says.

My heart sinks.

"Next week? Then you're leaving sooner than they said."

"No, they said be ready, that I could go any day. It could change again."

John's room is filled with equipment. I load his refrigerator with three of our homemade Tuscan egg pizzas, two roast chickens, fruit, and juice.

We go out with John's Marine buddy, Patrick. We sit in a bar and drink beer. John smokes. There is a band. The music is too loud to talk. I can tell he is relieved. What is there to talk about? We're just marking time till he goes. Everything has been said.

If we had an honest conversation it might go like this:

Me: "I'm sacred shitless."

John: "We've been through this. This is my job. Stop pissing and moaning!"

Me: "What did I do to make things turn out this way?"

John: "I thought you were proud of me!"

Me: "I am, but I wish this wasn't happening. When will you know where you're going?"

John: "I can't tell you that. Why *do* you keep repeating yourself?"

Me: "Because you've driven me *nuts*! Do you know what this is like?"

John: "Why are you so worked up? Why is this about *you*? *I'm* the one that'll get shot at!"

Me: "Wait till *you're* a father! Someday you'll know!"

John: "Yeah, yeah. . . ."

But we say nothing and sit silently nursing our beers, occasionally stealing a sideways glance at each other. The singer belts out old Beatles tunes from *Abbey Road*. John sits smoking, lost in thought. He has three beers and four cigarettes. Patrick has three beers. I drink two. If something happens to John, that stupid bar will be a shrine. I'll never listen to the Beatles again without crying. How weird in these circumstances, thirty-three years later, to hear the music that brought Genie and me together.

John has two beds in his small barracks room. I'm sitting on the spare bed. Next to me is the target John sighted his M-16 on. John shows me the nice tight grouping of the last four shots, the ones made after he sighted in. They are perfect, dead center on the torso of the man-shaped bull's-eye. Each bullet hole overlaps the next in an area smaller than a dime. John hasn't lost a step since qualifying as "expert" on the Parris Island rifle range. John hands the target to me.

"Here, Dad, you can have this," he says, and gives me a pat on the shoulder.

I carefully place the target in my bag. I hope if John is put in a lethal situation he kills whoever is threatening him before they kill him. I'd like to tell John that but I don't. I take some comfort in that tight dead-center grouping of shots.

I remember to tell John how much everyone at a recent reading I did from our book loved his poetry. I want to encourage him to write more poems while he is "over there." I don't want him slipping into an isolation he can't exit.

"The poems you wrote for *Keeping Faith* are a lot of readers' favorite parts."

"Thanks."

"I got a letter from a high school teacher saying she's reading them to her honors English class. You've got to keep writing."

"I will, but it isn't like boot camp—I mean, this is all classified."

"Okay, but about other stuff."

"When I can."

March 12, 2003

John and I have just come back from collecting his medical records. He's letting me tag along while he does his last-minute errands. On the way back to the barracks we pick up his desert uniforms, which have just gotten the name tapes sewn on. SCHAEFFER is on the name tape on the right side of his chest. US MARINES says the one on the left.

The Korean woman who runs the cleaners at one of the shabby strip malls (they seem to spring up like bad mushrooms around every base where I've visited John) glances at the cammies as we are about to leave.

"Good luck," she says quietly, in a heavy L-mangling accent.

I feel grateful. She noticed that John's cammies are for the desert. She knows what that means.

In the car John says, "The Koreans around here are all evangelical Christians, so everything is shut on Sundays while they're in church."

I try to talk some more, but he clams up. Maybe this wall between the one who is going and the ones being left behind is inevitable. John can't afford to be sentimental right now.

Holiday Inn at BWI [Baltimore airport]. I've been reading the *Financial Times,* killing time while John does what he needs to do alone to get ready. I read the newspaper distractedly. I'm hoping for a good last evening together. He's tired of my worried questions. He says so little. I wonder if his "it's all classified" isn't a convenient excuse for shutting down conversation.

At the end of the day I meet John. He has been getting briefings, shots, and filling prescriptions. He is "up." Back at the barracks he lays out his new acquisitions: three cases of Antidote Nerve Agent, Mark I (he is to inject one syringe into his right leg and the other into his left leg if he's hit by a nerve gas attack); antimalaria pills and antidiarrhea drugs (mild and superstrong) are in plastic bottles.

John had a rabies shot. His gas mask works and so does his rubber nerve-agent/gas protective suit. If they know a bio attack is coming, there are some pills to take. . . . Or is it if a chemical attack is coming?

"The big sand box" is how the other Marines refer to where John is going. They all act as if John is lucky and has won the lottery. They are jealous of his deployment. The Marines in intel vie for these interservice task-force missions the way athletes compete for a spot on a track team.

March 13, 2003

The anti-nerve-agent injections are on the table. Stacked next to the table on the floor is John's packed seabag. His Orthodox icons are on the wall. His prayer book is below them on the desk, along with his cammie cover [hat] presently being used as a holdall for his base security badge, his cigarettes and lighter, and his dog tags and Orthodox cross, which are on the same chain.

This second good-bye visit is reminding me of my dad's cancer. During the seven years it took him to die, each time Dad started to fail, the family flew to Rochester, Minnesota, where he was being treated at the Mayo Clinic. We came to say several "last" good-byes.

Then he'd respond to the therapy. A few months later we'd be back for another good-bye. I had at least three "last conversations" with Dad.

"Ted Turner told the employees of CNN that he'd never hire anyone dumb enough to smoke," I say, as John lights up outside his barracks.

"If he's so smart, why'd he marry Jane Fonda?" John answers with a grin.

The fruit I brought is stacked on the refrigerator. We eat some in the barracks lounge as we sprawl on the couches and watch TV, another excuse not to talk. John wears his polar bear pajamas, which I bought him as a goofy Christmas present four or five years ago. I find this weirdly comforting—a link to better times.

On the way out of the barracks we pass a young sailor.

"How's it going?" John asks.

"Busy saving the world one insignificant country at a time," she answers with a grin.

John and I laugh. Later John laughs again.

"What's so funny?" I ask, as we get back to his room.

"I was just thinking of a line I heard: What emotion is least likely to be found in battle?"

"Don't know."

"Whimsy," says John.

We both guffaw.

March 13, 2003

I'd write John a letter to take along but I don't want to unnerve him by making everything seem too final. He knows the depth of my love. I have this impulse to review our lives, to hold forth, give him a last lecture on all that is important. But I don't. In the face of his sacrifice, absolute honesty is demanded. And the truth is that over the years, much of what I've said to my children was somewhat—however unintentionally—false. I think I've pretended to be much more certain of my beliefs than I really am.

As a father it's been my job to present a world of order, right and wrong, and faith to my children. But now, on the cusp of this great divide, I can't play father any longer. I can only say what I know, that I love my son and am begging God to watch over him even though I sometimes lack the faith even to believe that God exists. I'll keep my mouth shut and, for once, not try to "teach" John anything. He is who he is now. Either some of what he's seen and heard has stuck or it hasn't.

A door is closing. The traditional father-son roles are about to reverse. I'm staying safe at home. My child is about to risk his life to protect me. And I'm powerless to help him.

March 14, 2003

I say good-bye to John at curbside at the airport. We pray together and I hold his hand. I make the sign of the cross over him and he bows his head. I bless him and work hard not to cry.

11

Friday, March 14, 2003 10:47 PM

We saw Billy off to Afghanistan last November and now he waits in Kuwait with 1st Fast Co. The emotions now are different and I have to catch myself before I think too hard about it all. Because your imagination takes you to places you do not want to be.

You trust in your son's strength, training, and the men he serves with. You trust in your country and its commander in chief. You remain strong and put up a fairly good front for your wife with confidence in how the boy will be fine! But then they see through us. . . .

Take care,

Alan D. Ross

Monday, March 17, 2003 8:06 PM

I can identify with John's impending deployment, as well as any trepidation that either he or you have relating to the deployment, including the looming threat of a war with Iraq. I was on active duty during the Gulf War in 1990–1991, and my unit deployed to the Persian Gulf. My unit (infantry) was part of one of the Marine task forces that spearheaded from Saudi Arabia up into Kuwait during the

100-hour ground war, which liberated Kuwait from the Iraqi troops.

John and your family are in my daughter's and my prayers nightly, and he has our undying support for his selfless dedication and service to our country.

Semper Fidelis,

Alan Hill

Former US Marine Corporal (infantry)

Tuesday, March 18, 2003 11:39 AM

Hello, Mr. Schaeffer. My name is Norma. My son is the Marine who recruited your son. Let your son know that we are saying a prayer for him . . . keep believing in him.

Sincerely,

Norma Dubois

March 18, 2003

Last night President Bush gave Saddam forty-eight hours to leave Iraq with his two sons or face war. I'm waiting for a call from John.

Yesterday afternoon I felt sick because I knew there were Marines, airmen, sailors, and soldiers now only a few hours away from the end of their lives. I could picture "my" Marines sitting in the desert, eating MREs [meals ready to eat], checking their equipment, nervous yet excited. Those about to die did not know that they would be the unlucky ones. In my imagination they all look like John and have his youthful sense of invulnerability.

Tuesday, March 18, 2003 12:59 PM

I was married to a career U.S. Army soldier for close to 20

years, but he is now retired. I am TOTALLY against this war, but I support our military personnel and their families unequivocally.

When I was living, working, and associated with active duty soldiers, I felt such a sense of pride, and naively thought the "outside world" supported the sacrifices we made on a daily basis. Now that I am . . . back in my hometown, far away from any military locations, I realize that no one really cares. Not really. . . . Oh, folks like to wave a flag around & wear pins & ribbons, but they consider military service someone else's job: someone who went into the military to stay out of jail, because they couldn't get a job anywhere else, because they aren't intelligent enough and don't have the skills to do anything else. . . .

My husband joined the Army during Vietnam to avoid the draft, plain and simple. But after serving, he changed his outlook completely. I had protested against the war in college, like everyone else, during the early 70s. Since I didn't grow up around any military facilities, I knew nothing about the people or the pride. . . . It's amazing what changes in outlook & perspective when you get to know our military personnel firsthand. . . .

Diane Long

Tuesday, March 18, 2003 1:15 PM

I am the mother of a U.S. Marine. . . . It is very hard for me to watch my son in the military, as I have a brother who is still listed as MIA from the Vietnam War and nothing has been heard of him since 1972. . . . Yes, we assume he is dead, but just the never knowing is very hard. . . . When my son chose the Marines over college I was very surprised, as he knew what my family has been through. . . . When his recruiter asked me what I thought of his decision, all I could reply was, "You really don't want to know what I feel and besides it has nothing to do with me. It is his life and I will stand by him no matter what he decides to do."

. . .

I only have one son and a daughter, and watching my son leave for Parris Island was extremely hard for me. . . . When I got to Parris Island to see him graduate I couldn't believe what a change I saw. . . . He left a boy and came back a very responsible young man. Now he is a dad and will someday understand all we have already been through. . . . May God be with your son and mine. . . .

Sincerely

Cherie Stevens

March 19, 2003

I cling to the rituals. I don't want to scratch under the surface. I want to believe John is serving in a perfect and worthy cause. I feel so lonely.

Wednesday, March 19, 2003 10:38 AM

Dear Papa, I think John is going to be too busy to get hurt. I hope he'll be on one of those huge bases or in some tiny isolated spot and he'll never see anyone. I hope his biggest problems will be a headache and boredom (sandstorms and bad food), not that those things aren't scary anyway. But we will pretend we are British and do a stiff upper lip for six months or so. When in doubt, fake it, being the motto of the day.

Love you,

Jessa [Jessica Schaeffer Strömbäck]

Wednesday, March 19, 2003 11:42 AM

My son was trained to be a Marine but I'm not sure how to be a good mother to a Marine. I haven't had any training for the things that are taking place now. I didn't think I would have to worry about him being in harm's way, but my 19-year-old Marine is on the front line. I was very much against his going into the military at first. He is also my youngest child. I want to try to understand more about his feelings. My daughter is engaged to a Marine—their wedding was to take place April 26th but we had to change that. . . . Her fiancé is on a ship in the Persian Gulf. . . .

My heart aches all the time. Just thinking about him over there is hard enough, but trying to talk about it is even harder. I am very proud of him and my son-in-law to be. Words of encouragement would be appreciated.

Thank you,

Susan Brown

March 19, 2003

John called.

"I don't want to upset you guys, but there are a couple of things I just wanted to settle before I go," John said calmly.

"Okay," I said.

Genie picked up the phone in her office.

"Hi, John."

"Hey, Mama," John said, and paused. "Well, as you know, Francis is the executor of my will."

"Right," said Genie quietly.

"So he should know all this, but I just wanted to go over it with you."

"Okay," I said. I was glad to be sitting, since my knees were suddenly feeling watery.

"If I don't come back I want to make sure the money from my life insurance gets spent right."

"Right," I mumbled.

"I'd like to, first of all, pay off all of Francis's college loans. Then I'd like to set up a trust fund for Amanda's and Benjamin's college, so once they get to that age they can go to school and it's all taken care of."

"I understand," said Genie.

"I want to be buried in Arlington, you know, if something happens. And make sure I have an Orthodox funeral. Oh, and if it happens, I don't want the Marines at Arlington doing the honors; try and get Marines from my own company to do it. I'd rather have the guys I know."

"Of course," said Genie.

"Now I'm going to call Grandpa Walsh and say good-bye, then go watch the war on TV, assuming it starts tonight."

12

U.S. Begins Attack with Strike at Baghdad
After Deadline for Hussein to Go Runs Out

March 20, 2003

The President went on the air to say it has begun. I feel as if my skin is missing a layer. I'm floating and my body has lost its bones.

4:26 AM. I sat up all night composing a letter to my friends and family. I'm sending this to make myself feel better, to do something, anything, to fight for my son and the choice he has made. I want to make sure people are thinking of him now.

To: All
From: Frank Schaeffer
Subject: My son is going to war
March 20, 2003

Before John joined the Marines my attitude toward our military was that of an editorial cartoon recently published in the *New York Times* (January 18, 2003). It was of a mock recruiting poster. The slogan ran, "OUT OF WORK?

UNDEREDUCATED? NO HEALTH PLAN? JOIN THE ARMY & SEE IRAQ."

To the *Times* editors this probably represented an ironic comment on the policies of an administration they hate. To me, as the father of a young Marine, it spoke unintended volumes about the condescending attitude that many of us harbor toward military service.

The sad thing is that before John joined I'd have read the cartoon and passed on with a shrug. Now it outrages me. Do you think that after 9/11 the *Times* would have printed a cartoon saying "OUT OF WORK? UNDEREDUCATED? NO HEALTH PLAN? JOIN THE NYPD & FDNY & DIE YOUNG."

It's been a long learning curve for me since John joined. General James L. Jones (Commandant of the United States Marine Corps, recently appointed chief of NATO) wrote to me about the affluent parents who find a child's unexpected choice to serve hard to bear. He wrote that "there has been a 'disconnect' between the men and women who defend our nation and those who are the beneficiaries of that service."

This "disconnect" is now so entrenched that there are a number of Americans who will not even allow their children's high schools to give their names and addresses to recruiters. Under the No Child Left Behind Act, schools are required to give the names, phone numbers, and addresses of graduating students to military recruiters unless parents request their children be omitted from the program.

A *New York Times* article ("Uncle Sam Wants Student Lists, and Schools Fret," January 29, 2003) quoted Donna Lieberman, executive director of the New York Civil Liberties Union, as saying, "Students have a right to not be bothered by aggressive military recruiters." In San Francisco's Contra Costa County, the article reported that school officials were looking for creative ways to thwart the law. Speaking of the requirement that his students hear a pitch from a recruiter, a Contra Costa board member was quoted as saying, "It's a dangerous precedent."

I envy my son's dedication and the brotherhood he shares with his fellow Marines. I am frustrated by the fact that we live in two Americas: one that serves, and one that doesn't. I admire my son's bigheartedness, born of service. As John is deployed, I am sad but proud.

Frank

I received dozens of responses, nearly twice as many as I sent, most from strangers who must have been forwarded a copy of a copy.

Tuesday, March 20, 2003 9:38 PM

I'm the first generation NOT to wear the uniform and sometimes I feel I didn't earn the freedoms I enjoy. I guess the idea is that they served so I wouldn't have to. That's what Dad always said.

This graduate-degree-holding Democrat has never had . . . [anti-military] attitudes. . . . Maybe it's because my Dad was at Pearl Harbor and my brother went to Vietnam. Maybe it's because of where we grew up—the heartland. All I know is that the service was never looked at as a safe option, but it was always a respectable one. . . .

Thinking of you all and praying for John.

Mark Wilder

Thursday, March 20, 2003 7:42 AM

If the unit your son is with over there is anything like my brother-in-law's unit, send books, magazines, and beef jerky. My brother-in-law's unit (from what he was saying) are literally reading just about anything they can get their hands on and the beef jerky can be used to barter with, so even if John doesn't like jerky he can get things from other guys with it (or so my husband was saying).

Amanda Boos

Thursday, March 20, 2003 6:43 PM

I write this e-mail from Washington, D.C., where I'm sitting at my desk on the 11th floor of an office building one block from the White House. I'm looking out at the Washington Monument through heavy rain and that sort of describes my mood. . . .

Our son, Frank Jr., is a captain and company commander in the 3RD LAR (Light Armored Recon) Battalion, which is now part of the 1st Marine Division leading the Allied forces into Iraq. You are probably feeling, as we do right now, that it may be harder to be back here in the States with your imagination running wild than to be over there surrounded by Marines who worry more about their comrades-in-arms than about themselves.

We (my wife and I) flew out to 29 Palms about six weeks ago to say good-bye and Godspeed to Frank, Jr., before he deployed. It was amazing. He could not understand why his mother was the least bit worried. He emphasized that his Marines were the best trained and most dedicated military men that he had been associated with during eight years in the military, including a year in Saudi Arabia as a Marine training the Saudi Army and six-months during which he did training exercises with armies from Great Britain, Italy, Israel, and Egypt.

His mother then questioned him on whether some of the antiwar protests that had started by then bothered him or made him bitter. He smiled. . . . First, he said that he was concerned that so few Americans really understood much of what is actually going on in the real world because they are so sheltered and privileged. Second, he said that one of the reasons he was going over to Kuwait, and wherever after that, was so people in this country—and hopefully soon thereafter in Iraq—could go out and legitimately protest their government's actions if they were so inclined. . . .

Francis X. Lilly

March 21, 2003

The news is war all the time. I realize I forgot to ask John if he can leave his stuff in his barracks room or if he has to pack it up. He still has no APO address we can write to. It's raining. Dirty snow is melting. We have no idea where he'll be. I like our new Subaru, but the fun of owning it is spoiled by the fact that John has never ridden in it. He grew up with the Taurus. There were plenty of scuff marks from his muddy soccer cleats on the back of the front seats. I don't want there to be things in my life John has never seen.

5:03 AM. I'm glued to the TV. . . . A Sea Knight helicopter has gone down in Kuwait. Four U.S. Marines and eight British Royal Marines died. I've been getting e-mails from mothers and fathers of many Marines. Today will be a day of grief and shock in four Marines' homes here and the homes of the eight British Marines in the UK. I'm sweating. I might throw up.

13

Thursday, March 20, 2003 4:50 PM
From: Frank Gruber
To: Frank Schaeffer
Subject: John and the war

Frank,

One thing before the first day of this war is over and before John ships out. Janet and I had a big discussion after Bush spoke. You know from my column that I believe the decision to go to war was immoral. Needless to say, that's one thing Janet and I agree about. But we also agreed that we didn't think that the fighting of the war itself was immoral, assuming, of course, that for any given individual, his or her conduct is lawful. We wondered why we instinctively believed that, given that "following orders" is no defense to war crimes and at first blush I would assume that goes for morality, too. I concluded that because what I thought was immoral was conduct at the political level—a superpower waging a preemptive war on its own say-so—the political immorality could not be attributed to troops who, after all, have a legal (and I would say moral) duty to stay out of politics. . . .

I mean, with John about to ship out, you might not care what we think of the war, but I want you to know how we feel—which is that we want the war to be as successfully fought as Donald Rumsfeld wants it to be fought.

All for now, love,

Frank

———————————

Friday, March 21, 2003 3:05 AM
From: Frank Schaeffer
To: Frank Gruber

Dear Frank:

I don't think you should use the words "moral" and "immoral." Where do these concepts come from in your naturalistic and secularized view of the world? Do you think that if the war is fought with international backing from the UN, that makes it "moral"? Does morality comes from a majority vote? When Hitler got the backing of 13 million voters, did this make his actions more "moral" than if he had not had a majority vote?

Why this trust in collective virtue and tidy legalisms? What makes multilateral "morality" any better than unilateral "morality"? Because the UN multilaterally decided to do nothing to stop the Rwandan genocide, did that make their inaction right?

As for John going to war, these are miserable days for Genie and me. It's 2:53 AM. I need sleep! I'm so tired but again I woke up with a jolt. It isn't just John keeping me awake; it's now knowing so many Marines personally who are in danger.

I could not face any of this without prayer. If you don't pray for Henry, then what do you do? And why do people want to pray, anyway? Why these longings for spiritual meaning? Again, if we are just part of nature, where in nature do we see the longing for meaning? The universe seems a mighty cold place to have produced such burning spiritual desire.

The inadequacy of hope vs. prayer is seen in our present situation. John is deploying to the Middle East to harm's way. You, as my friend, tell me "I'll be thinking of John." That is much appreciated. But other friends say, "I'll be praying for John." Your version of that is that you'll be "thinking of him." It is a religious impulse that has to find a respectable secular vehicle to express itself. But the thing that interests me is your impulse.

I find "I'll be praying for you" a more honest expression of human yearning. Your version is some kind of sanitized "seasons greetings," not much to fall back on in moments of suffering! I prefer that somebody prays for John than simply thinks nice thoughts about him, but I'll take that, too!

Best,

Frank

ALLIES OUTSIDE BIGGEST SOUTHERN CITY; FIREFIGHTS ON ROUTE TO BAGHDAD

March 22, 2003

John leaves tomorrow, Sunday. It was going to be Monday. Now it's Sunday night. I have the familiar ache in my loins. If I know Genie, she does too. We're overdue to go to bed together by several days. But tonight we each slink off to our own corners. I doze in front of the TV. She goes to her sewing room to putter around.

Frank mentioned he's having an Oscar party at his house tomorrow. Frank's friends in Santa Monica don't send sons and daughters to war. Ten thousand American servicemen and -women could be killed tomorrow night and for most of Frank's friends it would be nothing more than another headline, something interesting to speculate about that might help them get someone they like better than Bush elected as the next president.

The Republicans were no better. They were rooting for Clinton to fail in his international policy. But I truly believed presidents Clinton and Bush #1, when they wrote to me about their high regard for the military men and women they commanded.

I've discovered something: to have a child in uniform is to support the President in his role as commander in chief, whatever his politics.

———————

March 23, 2003

I couldn't sleep, even after taking my Tylenol and Benadryl. I blearily watched MSNBC all night. They had a live feed from Iraq. A British reporter was with our Marines. The Marines were in a fierce firefight near Basra, reported live, in real time.

An American soldier in the 101st Airborne threw two grenades into the tent where his commanders were resting. Two helicopters collided. Our soldiers mistakenly shot down a British warplane and killed the aircrew. My friend Frank is getting ready for his Oscar party. John goes tonight.

———————

Francis came to lunch. It was such a relief to see him! I'm feeling crazy with lack of sleep. I ranted about the Oscars going on in spite of the war.

"Dad, life goes on," said Francis.

"Yes, but Frank's friends would secretly rejoice at our losses!"

"C'mon, Dad, I don't think that's true. Most of the faculty at the Waring School is against the war, but they don't want John killed."

"They hate Bush more than they love our troops and would *love* to see the President get a black eye!"

"You're sounding a little, uh, over the top, Pop."

"Frank's friends know politics, but they don't personally know *one member* of the armed services! No beloved face springs to mind!"

"Maybe, but they still don't want John dead."

"I hope they choke on the salmon mousse!" I said.

"Time to bring back the guillotine, right, Dad?"

"What do they care?" I bellowed. "Elitist scum!"

"Dad, your idea of hardship is getting bad seats at the Metropolitan Opera!"

"Yeah, right, but my son's a Marine and you're a teacher, and I mow my own damn lawn! Anyway, what's wrong with going to the opera?"

Francis's teasing revived me, made me feel a little saner.

4:50 PM. Five minutes ago John called to say a last good-bye. He asked me to get his brother a hundred-dollar bottle of Scotch for Francis's thirtieth birthday, which John will miss—that and a joke present, the adult diapers Depends, for his "over-the-hill" big brother.

We've had so many false "last good-byes" that our actual farewell ritual was like an oft-repeated liturgical response. John was trying to sound as reassuring as possible, as if it were me who was facing the danger, not him.

"I love you, John."

"I love you, Dad."

"I am so proud of you, John."

"Thanks, Dad. But, Dad, I'm not doing anything terribly dangerous, so take comfort in that."

"Write soon," I said.

"I will, but, Dad, don't worry."

"John, watch yourself."

"I'll be careful."

"I love you, boy."

"I love you, Dad."

"Good-bye, John."

"I love you, Dad."

"Good-bye. I love you. Come back safe."

"I will, Dad."

———————————

I'm glad I was alone. I would not have wanted Francis to witness my coming apart. Francis and Genie said their good-byes on Francis's cell phone during a walk they took after lunch.

After I pulled myself together I spotted the photograph of my old movie producer friend John Kohn. I keep his picture tucked into the corner of the frame of one of Francis's childhood drawings. Big John K died a year ago in May. He served as a B-17 gunner in WWII, when aircrews mostly did not survive. I reached out and touched his picture, my icon of a loyal friend, one of the "greatest generation," a man who was the epitome of kindness. I felt comforted. John K would understand this moment. Best of all, he came home after facing far worse odds than my son is facing.

14

Allies and Iraqis Battle on 2 Fronts; 20 Americans
Dead or Missing, 50 Hurt

Monday, March 24, 2003 2:00 PM
Hello, Papa, how are you? I had a nice talk with Mom today,
sounds like John left in good spirits. Mom and I were exchanging
our own survival plans.

If it is any comfort I'm not sleeping well either. This morning
I just felt that getting the kids to school on time was one thing
too many on top of the war, so I let them sleep in and we had
a nice slow morning.

Love you,
Jessa

Monday, March 24, 2003 7:37 AM
From: Frank Schaeffer
To: Frank Gruber
Dear Frank: I'm tired and pissed off, pissed off with you
for watching the Oscars last night. One word: When reality

finally does break into the sunny clime you live in—sunny in every way—I hope for your sake you have more to hang on to than a never-ending lifelong meditation (dare I say compulsive fascination?) with what it means to be an agnostic.

Frank

Monday, March 24, 2003 4:37 PM
From: Frank Gruber
To: Frank Schaeffer
Subject: Your latest rant

Frank,

Okay, I watched the Oscars. Four of our closest friends came over with their kids. We switched the TV from CNN to ABC. I only checked the *NY Times* website once during the program.

If it's any comfort, everyone asked about John. No, we didn't pray for him, or you. I would say the mood among people I know—even Janet, who has the most reservations about us having gotten into the war—is: let's win this thing and hope the peace is a durable one.

I'm not sure what you want us to do. Ever since Korea the government and business have tried to persuade Americans that war and peace can coexist, at least economically—"guns and butter" it was called in the Vietnam era. The buildup to this war—from the Rumsfeld types—was that it would be over quickly, just like the first Gulf War.

I hate the attitude that war is heck, that we can go about our business, but you know, one of the officers who was attacked by the crazy Muslim G.I. was watching a golf video at the time. I think that's great—he had to take a break, and he did so.

I'm not going to take your bait about the "sunny clime" I live in. Not today, it's your day to be angry—and to know already everything I might tell you.

If that's rationalist and predictable, I'm sorry.

Frank

Monday, March 24, 2003 9:29 PM
To: Frank Gruber
From: Frank Schaeffer
Subject: You're a nicer friend than I deserve!

Dear Frank,

Okay, I know I'm being an ass! I have no idea what I want anyone to "do." My life has narrowed down to a single track. There is just this tunnel with John at the end of it. I have to admit that before he was deployed John had many of his buddies deployed and he was still watching TV, eating and laughing, as were all his fellow Marines. I'm not being rational or fair to you. I wish I had been there with you watching the Oscars myself! You all would have probably found that awkward.

Best,

Frank

Monday, March 24, 2003 8:31 PM

My husband is a Navy corpsman assigned to the Marines to provide medical attention. My husband decided to join the Navy Reserves 5 years ago. He wanted to serve his country. Now we sit as some of the members from his unit have been sent off. He longs to go and be with them, to help the fallen and wounded soldiers on the battlefield, but they have not called him yet. I sit and pray that if he goes God keeps him safe and brings him home to me and our two sons, Cody (6) and Jacob (4).

I come from a family drenched in the military spirit. As orphans in the Ohio Soldiers and Sailors home all 8 of my mother's brothers had to serve. Two served in Vietnam. . . .

This week has been very hard for our family. My oldest uncle's wife has been battling with cancer and as her fight neared to a close this weekend the family gathered. My uncles sat around the TV talking war and discussing what they can do to support our troops. They know what it is like and want our troops to maintain a good spirit. . . .

Please note that although your son is in battle, he is well taken care of by his fellow Marines and that if anything should happen to him the Navy corpsmen will fix him up.

Sincerely,

Leah Pittman

15

U.S. Copters Repelled: One Is Downed

March 25, 2003

I have been pickpocketed. I catch the thief and I am choking him and squeezing out his eye. I wake up. It's the first violent nightmare I've had in years. I slip into prayer, not elegant but repetitious and pleading, a child begging. "Please, please, *please!*"

They shot down a Cobra helicopter. They took our pilots prisoner. There are dark images on TV, on the front page of the *Times,* in my mind. There are POWs now, frightened American young people staring into the lens of the barbarian's camera.

I'm second-guessing every piece of advice I ever gave John, every book I ever gave him to read. Why are other kids sitting in safe classrooms and John is in his bulletproof vest? I'm proud of John and I'm wishing he were safe and yet I'm ashamed of that wish: should some other kid be doing this instead of mine?

Once, John said he wanted to be a priest. He was fourteen. I was just becoming aware of how difficult many Greek Orthodox priests' lives are. Some of them seemed so burned out, and when I talked to them, all they ever did was complain about their parish, their bishop, their salary, the jurisdiction they were in. I didn't want this life for John. I gave him a stern speech on how he had to be a lot more serious than simply mentioning that he might "like to be a priest." He never brought up the idea again. Another time we had a big fight over homework not done. I threw away his entire precious collection of Calvin and Hobbes comic books. Maybe he would have been a cartoonist or safe in some art school now if I'd let him keep those books. . . .

Last night Genie and I went to a Great Vespers service to celebrate the "name day" of our church, The Annunciation. The ancient prayers resonated, a source of comfort, a well-worn bridge to countless generations that have cried out . . .

Thou Who takes away the sins of the world, receive our prayer. Thou Who sits at the right hand of the Father, have mercy on us. . . .

We traipsed downstairs for coffee hour with the rest of the congregation. Everyone wanted to know how John was. Everyone was solicitous. They would pray for him, they all said. I repeated the same few lines again and again: "John is over there now. . . . No, we don't know where. . . . No, we don't know when he'll be back. . . ."

People seemed excited by the war. I used to watch wars on TV for the entertainment value too.

9:17 AM. I'm watching a military briefing. John calls from Germany. He flew over on a military charter. Tonight or tomorrow he will continue out to the Middle East on a military transport, probably a C-17, "hitchhiking" in the cargo bay.

9:42 PM. There are twenty Marines dead so far. This journal I'm writing is a monster version of John's and my book. It's as if *Keeping Faith* has come alive and is sadistically writing new chapters all on its own.

Some love can be written off as survival, as the passing on of our genes to the next generation, as selfish, as about no more than pheromones and rutting. But I'm starting to think that sacrifice and love are inseparable. In sacrifice we see proof of love being about something more than biology. When a child will risk death to protect his or her country, "love" is too small a word.

16

TROOPS ENDURE SLOWING SANDS AND MUD RAIN

ALLIES ADAPT TO SETBACKS

March 27, 2003

5:28 AM. "My Marines," as I now think of them, are in a gritty yellow-red sandstorm-choking hell. Men who hide behind children are shooting at them. Men who use hospitals and schools to hide weapons are attacking them.

I go downstairs and outside and rake the gravel off the lawn that was pushed there over the winter by the snowplow. Usually I greet spring with joy. I resent it this year. I want to plow under my garden to teach it that there is no business as usual!

7:10 AM. John called! He talked to Genie.

"How did he sound?" I asked.

"Tired, and I could hear other people around him," said Genie.

"When did he get there?"

"An hour ago. He said he couldn't talk and had to go."

"Well, at least he called. And he's all right! It took him, what, three, four days to get there?"

"Wherever 'there' is," Genie said.
"Did he hint where he was?" I asked.
"No. But he sounded like himself," said Genie.
I'll let the flowers live another day.

Thursday, March 27, 2003 12:55 PM

I read your book this winter and it prompted me to reread my father's war letters with new eyes. He served in the Army in World War II, and he was involved in North Africa, Sicily, D-day, and the Battle of the Bulge. Participating in ROTC at Stanford in the 1930s was an accepted thing to do in those days. . . .

It has taken me many years to comprehend and appreciate the sacrifices he made for our country. After the war, my father had a very successful career as a professor at Stanford. Yet I know that it was his experiences during the war that shaped his character and paved the way for success later on. My father and I have begun to talk about his experiences. I am so grateful to have this opportunity.

I grew up in the Stanford community in the 1970s, and the attitudes about military service you describe in your community mirror the attitudes I grew up with. There are many similarities between the San Francisco Bay area and the area around Boston, I think! But although I am disturbed by "knee-jerk" liberals whose view of the war in Iraq are completely colored by our experience in Vietnam, I am equally disturbed by those people I know who unquestioningly support the policies of the Bush administration.

My attitudes about the conflict in Iraq have been evolving. A few months ago a friend who has participated in the prewar peace demonstrations challenged me. "Aren't you worried about your sons?" she asked. "How will you feel if they are called into military service over this?" I just about astounded myself when I countered that I would be honored to have them serve. There was nothing more that she could say. We just chose to disagree. . . . I think that attitudes are changing towards military service, and it is going to take ordinary people like me to change them.

My 19- and 22-year-old sons show no interest in joining the military. . . . They are so prejudiced by their peers; I think that it would take a draft to get them to serve. . . . If my sons were drafted, I know that they would put their hearts and souls into the effort. They have a strong moral core of right and wrong. In fact, I think that military service would be of great personal benefit to them. . . .

I am very proud of our men and women in the military. I thank God for young people like your son. He is our best and I am so thankful for the sacrifices he is making on my behalf. I will pray for him.

Sincerely,

ERM

Thursday, March 27, 2003 6:29 PM

My wonderful husband, Jack, enlisted in the Army 15 years ago, when we were one of the poor white families you describe. In 15 years he has risen to the ranks of a Senior Noncommissioned Officer in the Army. He has deployed more than 24 times in 15 years and has defended his country with pride and determination. He hated leaving me and our four beautiful daughters at home, time and time again.

Jack has spent the last six months in Kuwait waiting on the war to begin. The night the war began, and every night since, I pray for his safe return and if not, the strength to sustain what may come to our family.

Since Jack's enlistment into the Army, I was able to go to college and am now the central support person for families and soldiers at the Great 3d Infantry Division at Fort Stewart, GA.

Here is what I have learned as an Army wife:

War is hell, both forward and at home;
America loves us (the military) when it suits them;
Asking for help does not mean you are helpless;
We are all created equal;
Children change your life;
Separations get harder the longer you have been married;
Maturity, not age, counts;
When the bad things happen, your family may get huge!
The military really is a small place. . . .

I will add you, your wife and your son to my prayer list. . . . Our soldiers didn't choose the fight; they only choose to give it their all.

Susan W. Wilder

Friday, March 28, 2003 12:49 PM

I am a 22-year-old college student about to graduate in approximately 6 weeks. . . . My heart is pulling me toward the Navy. My father was, or rather is, a Marine and he instilled much of the spirit of the Marine Corps in me growing up.

My college experience is a much different matter. I am an anthropologist. . . . An extremely liberal educational system and an even more radically liberal anthropological community surround me.

In my path toward the Navy I have been attempting to gather letters of recommendation and have hit a wall. Many of my professors have praised me as an academician but refused to write the recommendations for me on the basis that they are conscientious objectors. I have even been informed that I will never be truly accepted into the anthropological community after my service and should not hinder my future so much.

The truth of it is all of my school has been hostile toward the military. I have met more resistance in the past two months of exploring the possibility of commissioning than I have ever had to contend with before. . . . [I want to serve] my country against stereotypes as a woman serving in the armed services.

Thank you,
Stefanie Spradling

This story was everywhere today.

Columbia Prof Calls for Deaths of American Troops
Friday, March 28, 2003
New York (AP) — An academic furor was brewing Friday over a Columbia University professor who told thousands of students and faculty that he would like to see the United States defeated in Iraq and suffer "a million Mogadishus"— referring to the 1993 ambush in Somalia that killed 18 Americans.

The professor, Nicholas De Genova, told a "teach-in" on Wednesday "the only true heroes are those who find ways that help defeat the U.S. military." De Genova also asserted Americans who call themselves "patriots" are white supremacists. . . .

This anonymous e-mail was forwarded to me from an unknown source. I actually got five copies.

FW: To: NICHOLAS PAUL DE GENOVA

Fuck you, you fucking traitor! You are the biggest "Peace" of shit on this planet. May your body be dragged through the streets of NYC the way the bodies of our troops were dragged through the streets of Mogadishu!

The passions unleashed on both sides are nearing volcanic proportions.

17

March 29, 2003

7:50 AM. New York. Genie sits in bed reading the *New Yorker* and sipping coffee while I write. She has a business meeting here after lunch. Yesterday she wrote another note.

With John in harm's way when trouble comes, whatever form it takes—be it financial, personal, professional, religious—it either bothers me not at all, because I'm tired and numb, or too much, because I'm stressed and find even innocuous things threatening.

I can measure my stress in one way that seems silly in the grand scheme of things but that is "measurable" literally! Since the beginning of boot camp, my standard joke with John has been that as I worry about him and what hardships he might be going through, especially not having enough food, I start eating more! The summer before John started boot camp I probably weighed around 130. I don't know because my weight has never been a big issue for me. I judge my shape by how my clothes fit and adjust my eating accordingly. Before John joined, my weight was stable.

Since John went to boot camp, and especially since knowing he was to be deployed, my weight bobs up and down but mostly up. Is this a coincidence? He has been in four years; a lot can happen. I'm getting older and in the midst of menopause, so that doesn't help. But once John was deployed and worry became an everyday companion I started to comfort myself with food.

He has lost 15 pounds since becoming a Marine, which is the same amount I have gained. He gains his weight back each time he wants to. I can't seem to lose mine. It will be interesting to see, once he is out of the service, if I can achieve a consistent weight, get back my Marine son but lose my Marine pounds.

Central Park bench: waiting for Genie while she has her meeting. . . .

Taking a walk while Genie was in her meeting, I bought several *People* magazines. Ironically, we're in the "Oscar issue"! I flipped past acres of actresses in their twenty-thousand-dollar frocks, most of them wearing antiwar pins, and found John smiling at me from pictures taken when we horsed around in the snow behind our house for the photographer. I got a lump in my throat. I gave one copy to the doorman, Eddie, whose brother is in the Army. So far Eddie's brother has not been deployed. Eddie believes we are fighting for oil. So does most of the world. I don't believe that.

I don't believe the President, either, when he talks about the "weapons of mass destruction," let alone the "link" between Saddam and 9/11. I do believe that we're sending a long-overdue message. I agree with columnist Thomas L. Friedman. He says we must try to change the dynamic in the Middle East—that we can't just sit by passively and abet repressive backwardness forever. He says we're fighting a "revolutionary war of liberation" in Iraq and Afghanistan. I wish he were writing the President's speeches. I wish I knew if we will succeed.

I think that by not responding with vigor to Middle Eastern oppression or to the radical terrorist Islamism it helped spawn, many presidents, including Carter, Reagan, Bush #1, and Clinton, contributed to putting my son in harm's way. Treating the Israelis with kid gloves after they started building settlements on the West Bank, winking at the misogynistic brutality of the fascist Saudi regime while we sucked on their big oil tit, not declaring war on the Iranians after they took our hostages, running away from Beirut following the bombing of our Marine barracks, not finishing off Saddam in Iraq War I, and our hasty retreat from Somalia, when our choppers were shot down, did not save American lives, it sent the clear signal that we were soft and that if you hit us we'd run. This cost us three thousand lives on 9/11, a war in Afghanistan, and now another war in Iraq.

My heart sinks. Where is John right now?

March 30, 2003. New York City

Genie and I took the M-4 bus to the Cloisters. One of my favorite artworks there is *Standing Virgin and Child,* a small boxwood fifteenth-century sculpture by Niclaus Gerhaert von Leiden. John loves it. When I took John to the Cloisters for the first time he looked at the little sculpture for half an hour. He told me that he liked the way Mary cradles the child, her hand on the baby's soft wrinkled belly.

INFANTRY ATTACKS BAGHDAD DEFENSE WITH FIRST PROBES

IRAQI GENERAL SAYS 4,000 VOLUNTEERED FOR SUICIDE ATTACKS

March 31, 2003

Driving back to Massachusetts, I hear the news that three Marines have died in a chopper crash. My stomach cramps up. What three Marines?

When I hear about a specific Marine engagement, say with the 1st Marine Division, and there are casualties, I'm horrified but I know it's not John. When I can't rule out John, a sick feeling almost suffocates me.

I experienced this sense of suffocation once before. When we were still living in Switzerland, I left Francis, age five, playing in the yard with Jessica, age seven. I drove to the post office. Fifteen minutes later I came home. As I rounded the corner I saw a small knot of people gathered in front of my house. There was a car parked at an odd angle nearby. As I slowed I saw a child on the ground. The child was wearing a blue-and-white striped T-shirt, khaki shorts, and red boots, the clothes I'd dressed Francis in that morning.

There was blood. I crashed to my knees next to the child just as a sobbing woman turned him over. It wasn't Francis. The boy was the same size as my son and dressed in the same outfit. Relief flooded over me. I helped the mother get her son into the ambulance, put her in my car, and we followed.

News of each Marine killed makes me feel as I did during the eternal thirty seconds when I thought Francis was the child facedown in a spreading pool of blood. Maybe it's only for a few terrible seconds. Maybe it's a time-stopping hour, or even half a day before I know it isn't John, but every announcement that begins, "Today a Marine was killed . . ." drains the life out of me.

I'm worried that John might hesitate to use lethal force. I fear his innate kindness. Some Marines were killed three days ago because they stopped to help a man with his car. He blew himself up and killed them.

The first Marine killed in Operation Iraqi Freedom fell in an attack by Iraqi soldiers hiding in a civilian vehicle, some masquerading as civilians. Lieutenant Jane Vizzi Blair knew the fallen hero.

Tuesday, April 1, 2003 12:17 PM

Frank, I went to the Basic School with Lt. Childers. He was the first Marine killed in this war.

He was a great Marine and did everything from embassy guard duty in Kenya, to leading his Marines into battle in Iraq. Lt. Childers went into the Corps right out of high school, just like John. He served 12 years, first as an enlisted Marine then, after participating in the military scholarship program for bright gifted Marines—he went to college (the Citadel) where he made the dean's list—he went to officer school at the same time as me. Lt. Childers died during his first combat mission.

Jane Vizzi Blair

[Lt. Therrel Shane Childers was in unit 1 Battalion, 5th Marines, Alpha Company. Date of death was 21 March 2003. 2nd Lt. Childers was killed during enemy engagement in Rumaylah. He and his platoon fought the Iraqi troops while securing a burning oil pump station in southern Iraq. They were in the consolidation phase, still holding security when a truck came driving from the south. There were Iraqis in the back with weapons that began opening up on the Marines. Lt. Childers was hit from the initial enemy fire. Lt. Childers was buried in Powell, WY.—FS]

18

April 1, 2003

There was a postcard from John today! It was mailed from Germany, where he had changed planes. On the front was a fat man in lederhosen with a tuba. On the back a hastily scrawled note:

"Silly Germans. I'm doin' fine. Love, JLS"

Genie and I repeated John's words ten times or so, laughing over the coded "silly Germans" message. It alluded to one of John's favorite episodes of *Fawlty Towers*, the "Germans Episode," as we call it. I telephoned Francis and told him we'd heard from John.

"Basil Fawlty!" Francis laughed.

"The Germans Episode!" I laughed.

" '*Don't* mention the war!' " Francis said, quoting our favorite line.

"Silly Germans!" we bellowed together.

"He sounds fine," said Francis.

"Just like himself!" I exulted. "Kidding around."

The TV is full of antiwar, anti-American demonstrations. Genie said—dejectedly—that the lack of support for our troops here at home is getting her down. I told her there was support for them. She said, "Not in the *Times* and not on NPR. They seem so distant from our soldiers."

Tuesday, April 01, 2003 1:32 AM

Papa, Thanks for the e-mail. How great to hear from John. Silly Germans indeed! I keep thinking that this will all be over someday, but when a twelve-day war starts to feel an age, one wonders. Oh well, usually things develop; and if we get some more news from John our state of mind will improve dramatically. Our guys are doing a really impressive job though. I am so proud of them.

I am off to glaze my next batch of tiles.

Love you,

Jessa

19

IRAQ IS PLANNING PROTRACTED WAR

ARAB VOLUNTEERS SEEK TO JOIN FIGHT AGAINST U.S.

Stir Continues over Columbia Professor's Comments
Wednesday, April 2, 2003

NEW YORK (AP)—The controversy over a Columbia University assistant professor who called for the bloody defeat of U.S. troops in Iraq refuses to die, with critics heaping scorn and supporters saying he has gone into hiding after receiving numerous death threats. . . . The threats led De Genova to nix his two classes on Tuesday, according to the student newspaper. . . . Some students defended the professor. About two dozen of his students took part in a silent protest on Tuesday, as they sat quietly outside in the rain to show their support of De Genova. . . .

April 4, 2003. Evansville, IN

An e-mail message from John! Brief and to the point! And, best of all, current, not days or weeks old like the card. I'm sitting in a hotel room when I read it off my laptop. I have to look at the words a dozen times to be sure it's really him.

———

From: John Schaeffer
Thursday, April 03, 2003 4:18 PM
Subject: Hey everyone,
    How's it going, hope everyone's doing well, I'm fine. Just thought I'd drop you a line to let you know that I'm doing fine—don't really have time to write, very busy.
    All my love,
    JLS

I called Genie. She went online and found John's e-mail too. My spirits lightened. I called Francis and rejoiced with him, e-mailed Jessica, then called Frank. He was delighted.

20

April 5, 2003

4:37 AM. Some Orthodox Christians calling themselves the "Orthodox Peace Fellowship" [a group based in The Netherlands] have circulated an e-mail antiwar declaration—not just anti this war but anti *all* war; therefore, by extrapolation, antimilitary and anti–Cpl. John Lewis Schaeffer, USMC, the kid who gave up soccer practice to serve faithfully as an Orthodox altar boy for nine years!

[In October 2002, a ten-person self-appointed "council" drafted "A Plea for Peace," which 146 persons had signed by March 19, the first day of the U.S.-led intervention in Iraq. A gaggle of American Orthodox bishops, prominent laity, and priests—from the Greek, Russian, and Arab Orthodox jurisdictions—signed this document.—FS]

Corporal John Schaeffer, USMC, wore his Orthodox cross into battle and took his icon of Saint George with him, the same sweat-stained icon he carried in his cammie pockets through boot camp. The last thing John asked for before he left was an Orthodox burial if he is killed serving his country. I didn't expect some bishops and priests to stab him, and all other Orthodox Christians serving their country, in the back.

The peace letter calls soldiers "murderers," albeit in a roundabout, disingenuous way. It accuses my country—the country that gave most of the signers (or their parents) refuge from persecution by the Turks, assorted Muslim tyrants, and the Soviets—of using "any means" to overthrow Saddam. They speak of America as one might speak of the Nazis.

> "The United States is ready to overthrow him [Saddam Hussein] by any means, including an attack which would kill thousands of civilians and maim many more. . . ."

The United States manifestly is *not* ready to overthrow Saddam by "any means." That lie should have stopped any responsible (or honest) person from signing his or her name to this garbage! We could carpet bomb the cities the way the Russians do in Chechnya, but instead we're risking the lives of our soldiers by performing surgical air strikes against government buildings and avoiding civilian casualties at all costs. Lieutenant Childers would be alive if he had ordered his men to just blast that civilian pickup truck when he first saw it. But he didn't.

> "The Orthodox Church has never regarded any war as just or good, and fighting an elusive enemy by means which cause the death of innocent people can be regarded only as murder. Individual murderers are treated by psychiatrists and priests and isolated from society. But who heals the national psyche, the wounded soul of a nation, when it is untroubled by the slaughter of non-combatant civilians?"

If the signers claim to believe the Bible, they are calling God a murderer. The Scriptures say God commanded certain wars and even punished his people for not prosecuting them with enough vigor. Maybe there is no God or maybe he is evil, but the Orthodox Church has never said so. There are good arguments for pacifism, but they certainly can't be found in the Bible, not when the book is taken as a whole.

We Orthodox venerate some saints who were pacifists. We also venerate some saints who were soldiers and continued to be soldiers after their conversion to Christianity. The Church asks for peace in its prayers but has never contradicted the Apostle Paul, who wrote that the state does not "bear the sword in vain." The Orthodox Church includes specific prayers for our soldiers and military personnel in our liturgies alongside pleas for peace. Has the Church been praying for the success of "murderers" for two thousand years?

"If the world can be convinced that it's possible to work peacefully to make life more livable for all, we will all be better off. This is the reconciliation we hope for as Christians among individuals. Can it not happen among nations, between Iraq and its neighbors, and for all the good people of the world?"

What is the authors' and signers' answer to Saddam's torture chambers, Pol Pot's killing fields, Auschwitz, the gulags, the Taliban's whips, the Rwandan genocide, misogynistic Islamic fascism, international terrorism, and 9/11? Be nice and hope tyranny, violence, murder, and oppression just go away. . . .

Genie had been listening to my fuming about the peace letter. A few days before I had asked her if she thought I could craft an op-ed as a response. She smiled.

"Yes, but you need to come off as minimally rational. Just try and *pretend* you are," she said with a laugh.

Stripped of Spiritual Comfort
by Frank Schaeffer
The Washington Post, Sunday, April 6, 2003

A few weeks ago my wife, Genie, and I got the news that our Marine son, John, would shortly be deployed to the Middle

East. He is gone to war now. We have been dreading this moment. We don't dare go for a walk. What if he should call? I wake with a sickening jolt each dawn.

Genie is quieter than usual. I snap at her over small things. The ground feels brittle under my feet. My one comfort has been prayer and church. Now I'm feeling forlorn even about going to church.

I am a member of the Greek Orthodox Church. Some Orthodox Christians calling themselves "The Council for the Orthodox Peace Fellowship in North America" have circulated an antiwar declaration harshly condemning the U.S. government's policies in Iraq. In this "peace statement" the authors call all soldiers who kill in battle murderers, no matter what the cause. They accuse our country of using "any means" to overthrow Saddam Hussein.

I don't agree with the authors, and I believe they have simplistically misrepresented the teachings of my church. But that is not the point. They are entitled to say or believe anything they want, as individuals and private citizens.

I am saddened because so many of my bishops and priests have signed this antiwar statement in the name of my church and my God. They have dragged not only my church but Jesus into their stand against our government and the war in Iraq.

It is cruel to try to hijack the authority of a church to advance political views for or against this war. I would never sign a letter for a "Council for the Orthodox Pro-War Fellowship" just because my son is serving his country in the military. I'd assume that it would be preposterous for me to speak for my fellow Orthodox Christians on such matters of individual conscience, over which honest and honorable people can disagree.

How excluded from spiritual comfort the Roman Catholic

parents of our young service men and women must feel now that the Pope and so many American Catholic bishops have condemned our government's policies in the name of their church. The same lonely sadness must be felt by the parents of soldiers from the mainline Protestant denominations, whose leaders have condemned the war in Iraq and our commander in chief in the name of their churches.

I don't see my son as a murderer. I don't see my country as evil. I see my country and my son's cause as just. But maybe I'm wrong. If I'm wrong I don't want to drag God down with me. I don't claim that Jesus is on my side. I'm hoping that God is on the side of my pacifist friends too. And I assume God is hearing the prayers of Iraqi parents worried about their sons who are serving their country.

How can a church comfort all its children when it plays political favorites? I believe that the Greek Orthodox whose sons and daughters are marching in peace rallies should find as much comfort in our beloved church as I do. I don't want them excluded or condemned in the name of God. Yet as the father of a Marine I feel excluded from my church at the very moment when I most desperately need to be included. Why have so many priests and bishops traded their call to pastoral care for a few fleeting moments of political "relevance"?

My son is gone to war. I am sad and frightened. I am also proud of my Marine for his selfless service. But I am being stripped of the comfort of my church in the name of "peace" by people who seem determined to make God as small as we are.

21

ALLIES PRESS BAGHDAD

18 DIE AS U.S. AIRSTRIKE MISTAKENLY HITS KURDISH FORCE

April 7, 2003

A friendly Greek Orthodox priest from Indianapolis extends his pastoral care. He writes: "I am one of the signers of the Orthodox Peace Fellowship Iraq appeal. . . . I think it's unfortunate that you choose the emotionalism of your son's combat service to advance the new book [about him], which 'coincidentally' just recently came out. I'm sure . . . your *Washington Post* tirade won't hurt sales of your book. . . . The military puts its best efforts into making our servicemen into killing machines. . . . [Our] putative president . . . represents the ruling plutocracy of our nation and is using our largely blue-collar, southern, and minority frontline troops as so much fresh meat in the meat grinder of his imperialistic ambitions."

Another fan writes in the liberal spirit of ecumenical dialogue: "You seem not to understand the simple purpose and message that was Christ's life. . . . Perhaps I can refresh your memory. Jesus was about peace and love. . . . As a Catholic, I, for once, am gladdened that MY church (i.e., the Pope and many priests) have demonstrated the backbone to speak against this criminal invasion. . . . Yes, Jesus was/is a radical and you seem to be the kind of person in the crowd throwing stones at Him for challenging the status quo."

I get many other e-mails, most of which are positive.

Tuesday, April 08, 2003 3:33 PM

The people who call themselves peace activists (while screaming abuse) but claim to "support the troops" are very much like the people who picket abortion clinics and scream, "BUT WE LOVE YOU!" at the women whose paths they impede. I don't think the troops feel supported any more than those women feel loved. . . .

Take care—

Mary Gibbons

PS—If you are having trouble eating because you are worried or stressed, try baby food bananas. Gross, it's true, but they're easy to eat and will keep you going!

Monday, April 07, 2003 2:46 PM

Amen! I am Methodist . . . the United Methodist Council of Bishops issued a similar statement before hostilities began in Iraq. . . . I . . . believe our so-called Christian leaders have crossed a line that indirectly supports brutality, terrorism, and dictatorial totalitarian anti-Christian types of governments. . . . How dare they?

Thank you for your statement.

L W

Monday, April 07, 2003 1:30 PM

I am not Greek Orthodox; in fact, religiously we could not be further apart. I am Jewish. But I have a Marine daughter and a 16-year-old Flower Child. I am proud of both. . . .

The problem with religious [people] is they feel a need to express only one view whereas in life most situations warrant many possibilities. I wonder what your [church] might feel if told that their inaction makes them part of the problems. . . .

Mind you, I do not believe in war but I do believe in freedom for all human beings.

Maureen Landau

Monday, April 07, 2003 4:50 PM

It is a horrible thing when the Church makes such a statement, whether it is Orthodoxy, Roman Catholicism, or the Presiding Bishop of the Episcopal Church stating that he is tired of having to apologize for being an American. I am afraid, however, that it will ever be thus. As a chaplain serving in Viet Nam, I was described as having "left ministry."

I continue to pray for John, and for all the others who are in harm's way.

Victor Krulak

Monday, April 07, 2003 1:44 PM

I am certain you know there are many Greek Orthodox priests who support America and her troops. Father Anthony Kosturos of San Francisco is our parish priest and had been a great source of support for all those who serve. . . .

Sincerely,

Anthony Kakis

Tuesday, April 08, 2003 12:01 AM

My wife and I read your article and she exclaimed, YES! She subscribes to the *National Catholic Reporter*. Several recent editions have carried comments by priests and peace activists

113

condemning our troops and even going so far as to say that our troops should be denied Communion. . . .

Tom Puplava

Monday, April 07, 2003 12:46 PM

You might look at attending services at a military chapel—one of the services may have a base or post near where you live. . . .

Take care,

Mac and Linnea McIntosh

Monday, April 07, 2003 9:51 PM

Although some people in your church will turn their backs to us, remember that is OK. The only person that can look down on a MARINE is God.

Semper Fi

Danny Brock

Sgt., USMC

22

U.S. Blasts Compound in Effort to Kill Hussein

Stubborn Resistance for Marines

April 8, 2003

A letter from John just arrived! He sent it almost two weeks ago. There's a red dusty thumbprint on it, and the pages are gritty with powder-fine sand.

March 28, 2003
Arrived here yesterday, things going pretty well. I'm starting work tonight; think I'll be working nights for the rest of the time I'm here. This is my address: —————————
One thing: Under *NO* circumstances put my rank on the envelope. I need you to send me some money. No ATM's in this country, ya know, locals won't take credit cards for some reason! About $300. Just take the money out of my account. Work will be very interesting. Will be doing good things. Can't write much right now. Busy.
Love, JLS

———————————————

Public Seems to Tolerate the Level of American Casualties

Tuesday, April 08, 2003 12:16 AM

I am very happy for you that you have heard from John. It must have brought you and Genie some degree of comfort. Still no word from Jason since the war began. Every time I hear of a Marine being killed, my heart sinks and I wonder if the uniformed men will show up at my doorstep. When they don't, I have a fleeting moment of relief that is quickly replaced by the realization that some other parent is feeling the extreme anguish I so fear. In that respect, I believe we military parents are all connected.

God be with you and yours,

Laura Taylor

(Marine Mom)

23

April 9, 2003

Baghdad falls. Oprah calls. This is the strangest day of my life.

In a wanna-be-a-manly-man-and-support-our-troops mood (and maybe slightly unhinged by the news I'll be on *Oprah*), I made a grand gesture while Genie watched in disbelief. I stripped to my underpants on a lonely stretch of Plum Island late this afternoon to bodysurf. A steady wind was blowing. The water was testicle-shrinking-to-the-size-of-frozen-peas frigid. The air temperature was about forty-five. There were still patches of snow in the hollows of the dunes.

"What are you doing?" asked Genie.

"John Kohn loved to body surf, and the waves are perfect!"

"And?"

"I want to pay tribute! He died in May!"

"This is April."

"Oh?"

The last light of day stained the water a pastel silvery mauve-blue. I felt as if I were melting into the sky. Hypothermia will do that, make you feel peaceful and one with nature. . . .

"Come out *now!*" called Genie. "You've proved your point!"

117

"*What 'point'?*" I yelled back over the roar of the surf.

"*I have no idea!*" Genie yelled back.

"C-Corporal John Schaeffer l-loves to bodysurf t-too! I w-want to enjoy the moment for both of them!" I called through chattering teeth.

The pain from the cold was spreading up my legs, from feet that felt as if they had just been struck by a hammer.

"John Kohn went bodysurfing in *California*! And John Schaeffer knows you're nuts! COME OUT NOW!" commanded Genie.

I stayed in five minutes longer—just to show Genie I'm strong—got a couple of good long rides, then staggered out shivering and kissed her. Genie's lips felt beautifully warm against my frozen mouth. I wanted to hang on to that moment, too, but icy water was dripping off me so she stepped back and handed me her sweater to dry off with.

"Next time at least bring a towel," said Genie.

"You have to b-be more s-s-spontaneous. How could I know this would be the right thing t-to do before we got here?"

Genie rolled her eyes.

"John Kohn was the best person!" I said.

"So you dive into the Atlantic?"

"A soul longs f-for-forever!"

"You're turning purple."

"Our longing for immortality is horrible! Death sucks!"

"This revelation came to you in the water?" Genie asked, as she helped me get dressed.

"Yes."

"When that big wave tossed you on your head?"

"We want to live forever! Dogs don't want that!"

"They don't go bodysurfing in winter, either," Genie said as she helped me pull on my shirt.

Wednesday, April 09, 2003 9:03 PM

We heard from Peter last night. He called during dinner, so we all got to talk to him. He called via a satellite link from Iraq somewhere, so we had static and lags in conversation. He sounded great and very upbeat. His favorite words were "I am not at liberty to say."

He said to say thanks to everyone for the support.

Michael Kirby

Thursday, April 10, 2003 12:30 PM

I just wanted you to know that I received e-mail from Tom this morning. He still doesn't say where he is. . . . He sends his love to all. He said he's been receiving your letters and cards. He has not received boxes as yet. I understand there is a huge stockpile of boxes and packages to be delivered to the troops when they can. . . .

Thank you for your love and support.

Grace M. White

April 10, 2003

The dirty snow on the ground matches my mood. Oprah *is* going to have me on—along with some other military parents—to talk about our sons and daughters. I should be glad. I'm excited at the possibilities for our book, but this is all out of sync. They found bloody American uniforms yesterday in a prison in Baghdad. I have no idea where John is.

Genie was taking a nap and I bellowed up the stairs, "It's JOHN!"

He sounded tired and calm. We asked him how he was. Was he eating? Sleeping? What could we send him?

I grabbed a notepad and began to scribble furiously. Knowing that Jessica and Francis would want it word-for-word, I tried to write down the nuggets. I knew the call would go by fast and that John had a lot to say in a short time. Our biggest question was, Where the hell is he? But Genie and I had learned not to press. . . .

"How are you?" asked Genie.

"I'm fine."

"Are you getting any sleep?" she asked.

"I'm sleeping in a tent and working mostly nights. It's very hot in the day, so I wake up sweating."

"How come?" I asked.

"Because in the desert it's cold at dawn when I go to sleep, so I need the sleeping bag."

"Are you safe?" asked Genie.

"I sleep well, except when a mine explodes. We have to be in the middle of the biggest minefield in the world."

"What!" we both exclaimed.

John chuckled.

"Don't worry, people watch the perimeter. Our guys are serious," John said with another chuckle, "I'd be willing to pay to do this job."

"What can you tell us about your work?" I asked.

"It's important stuff and affects day-to-day life for people. We do bad things to bad people. . . . And if I could, I'd work twenty-four hours a day."

"Day-to-day, where do you go?" I asked.

"Sometimes out, then we return to base. The big news is that I can tell you where I am right now. I'm in Afghanistan."

"Wow!" I said.

"Oh my!" said Genie.

"I had something to do with some interesting things recently, just a little part. I got to see some of our prisoners the other day. The clever bad guys are still out there. . . ."

There was a roar in the background. John paused.

"D'you hear that? That's an A-10 going over. . . ."

There was a big rumble.

"We're in a heavily mined area, mostly old Soviet mines. This call will cut off in a few seconds. Don't worry when it does. I think a camel just blew up. The Russians mined everything out here! Crazy. . . ."

"What about food?" I asked. "What can we send?"

"We're fine, maybe gummy bears."

"We love you!" said Genie.

"Everyone is so proud of you! WE LOVE YOU!" I bellowed.

The phone went dead. I raced upstairs.

"He's in *Afghanistan!*"

"Yes," said Genie with a frown. "And isn't it *so typical* that he eased into the big news!"

We both smiled.

"Do you think that makes him safer than if he were in Iraq?" asked Genie.

"I don't know. They're rounding up Taliban and Al Qaeda. . . ."

"I still feel relieved to know where he is, though," Genie said, and thought for a moment. "The question is, is he putting on all this cool bravado for us so we won't worry, or is John really feeling that way?"

"Good question," I said.

I called Francis. "At least now we can worry specifically," he said.

"That's just what I was telling Mom," I said. "I'm so glad you're around. It's a big comfort having you close by."

I called Jessica and woke her up. I read her my notes of what John said.

"Man, is he crazy or what?" Jessica said, and laughed.

"He sounded so calm and enthusiastic! Did we raise him differently from you and Francis?"

Jessica laughed.

"I mean, can you picture either of you doing something like this?" I asked.

"No."

"Well, where the hell does this kid come from?"

"He's great, isn't he, Papa?"

"He sure is," I said.

My eyes suddenly filled with tears. I hung up and thought about how unexpectedly tears come these days. This must be the way women feel when they have those postpartum blues. I'll start a thought smiling and end it tearing up. Even sappy commercials choke me up! Genie is going through menopause on top of this war and she's keeping it together better than I am! But then, I don't know what she does when she gets up at odd hours and wanders alone. In the mornings I find her sleeping on John's bed.

April 11, 2003

My friend Frank Gruber just arrived from California. He is going to stay with us for a few nights while he goes to events at his Harvard Law School alumni reunion. Frank is pleased for us that at last we know where John is. We discuss if John is safer in Afghanistan than he'd be in Iraq.

"All of life is dangerous," says Frank. "I'm sure he'll be fine."

It's good to have Frank here. I'm hoping some of his sensible, calm optimism rubs off on me.

Friday, April 11, 2003 6:30 PM

I am a foreign service kid, raised in the 60s & 70s in the Horn of Africa; an Embassy Marine (try Geneva, Switzerland!); a Fundamentalist Christian (1980); have been through a couple of schools at Fort Huachuca; and finally, a retired United States Marine (23+ years). . . .

Twice I was asked to pony up, Gulf 1.0 and Somalia. My bets came all too close to getting called, but here I sit some years later, knowing the brother I love so deeply, the other son of my parents, is now in harm's way; I will tell you, this is harder. . . .

When I was most scared, when the tracers were so close I could smell them, could have reached out to be touched by them, when I was pressed so low to the ground that it hurt, I was not alone. In a physical sense, yes, my world became a very small circle, and I was naked and alone in the middle of that circle. But my fear was held and banked by Someone else being there with me, giving me comfort when I certainly needed it most, at the bottom of the valley. . . .

Mr. Schaeffer, I encourage you to remember the motto you learned from your son: *Semper fidelis.* In only a slightly different context, it can be translated "Keep the Faith."

Jeffrey R. Climer
Master Sergeant of Marines (Retired)

24

We got an e-mail from John. It was a poem. For the first time since he left I feel as if he's in the room with me, that I'm hearing his real voice.

tired country
old and tired country
with a spark of hope now
maybe a rebirth

25

April 12, 2003

4:27 AM. The war in Afghanistan is "John's War" now. His war is heating up. The Taliban and Al Qaeda are regrouping in Pakistan. There are cross-border killings almost every day. From the beginning of John's deployment, even when I thought he was in Iraq, I've feared terrorism more than a straight-up fight. I pray he's not in the wrong place at the wrong time.

———

10:54 PM. Genie informs me her father has cancer on his vocal cords. She said nothing about it while Oprah's camera crew was here even though Pam [Genie's sister] called her earlier in the day. I tell her to make sure she tells John to stop smoking next time he calls, that the genes in our family will kill him if he doesn't quit. Dad died of cancer and now her dad's got it too. She went up to bed alone.

I morosely watch TV, feeling depressed. Stan Walsh has cancer and all I said to Genie was to tell John to stop smoking! I didn't hug her or commiserate. Now Genie is asleep and I let her go to bed, without apologizing for being such a jerk.

———

April 11, 2003

BAGHDAD (AP Wire Service)—Marine Cpl. James Lis, 21 years old, is worried that for the rest of his life he'll be haunted by the image: A clean-shaven, twentysomething Iraqi in a white shirt, lying wounded in an alleyway and reaching for his rifle—just as Cpl. Lis pumped two shots into his head.

"Every time I close my eyes I see that guy's brains pop out of that guy's head," Cpl. Lis, from Shreveport, La., told his platoon mates Thursday, as they sat in a circle in the ruins of the Iraqi Oil Ministry's employee cafeteria. "That's a picture in my head that I will never be able to get rid of."

And of course I wonder, What is John seeing?

Saturday, April 12, 2003 11:49 PM

I'm glad John has the opportunity to do what he's doing. We're lucky in our MOS [Military Occupational Specialty] that we usually are working a real-world mission whether in peacetime or wartime. I know you're worried about him but what he's doing now really is the epitome of what he's trained for. . . . I'm really happy for him.

My husband, John, returns from Kosovo on 21 April, but I'm sure he'll be redeployed to Iraq to aid in the civil-military affairs mission that will probably last quite some time.

I'm glad that you're busy, since it probably helps that nagging concern for your son's safety that's ever present in your head.

Take care,

Mary Kay Church

[The writer is an officer in the USMC, as is her husband.—FS]

Saturday, April 12, 2003 9:45 PM

At this moment the wife and I are getting a little queasy, as we have not heard from Billy for one week. When Cyndi talked to him last Saturday, I was at work. She said that they had been instructed to be ready to move out at a moment's notice. . . .

I guess we will have to keep tag-teaming support back and forth for a while longer, eh?

Take care,

Alan D. Ross

April 13, 2003

3:20 PM. Genie and Francis are out for a walk. Frank Gruber just left for the airport.

Frank seemed constrained during his visit. We hardly argued, had only two minor skirmishes over my contention that the phrase "secular Jew" is an oxymoron—"Frank, if there is such a thing, can I convert to be one?"—and Frank's contention that the American flag has been "taken over by the right."

Strange that with John gone to war we still fight through our e-mails but face-to-face we were so intimidated by the war we hardly dared argue. Being polite to Frank was very unsettling, as if we were observing decorum at a wake. However, I cooked him a great seven rib pork roast—lightly hickory smoked and glazed with a peach-soy reduction.

John just called! I took notes for Jessa, Francis, and Genie.

"You should see what the Taliban and Al Qaeda did to this country, especially to girls who wanted to go to school. They whipped women who didn't dress right and shot men who didn't grow beards. . . . This is the most satisfying work I've ever done."

"Can you be more specific?" I asked.

"I can tell you pieces of what we do, because it's not all classified, but not over the phone. . . . Well, I got to get back to work, as my OIC [officer in charge] says we're 'driving the fight' right now. . . . I took pictures during a trip today, pretty cool pictures, and will send the camera to you next week. . . . Working sixteen to eighteen hour days or more. . . ."

While I was still on the phone with John, Francis and Genie came back from their walk. I handed Francis the phone so the brothers could speak. Francis hasn't talked to John since he left.

John called back twice so he could talk to his brother longer. I think one perk these intel guys have is access to some pretty sophisticated mobile communications equipment in the field.

After the call Francis said John told him that a remote-controlled mine was placed next to the road he was driving down. John told his brother about the IED [improvised explosive device]. I guess I know why he chose not to tell me.

26

Sunday, April 13, 2003 2:00 PM

Hello Papa, how are you? I had nice a talk with Mom today, sounds like John was in good spirits. We were exchanging our own survival plans. If it is any comfort I'm not sleeping well either. Taught my art class tonight. We are doing a series on Egypt. Going to go kiss Amanda and Ben good night. . . .

Love you,

Jessa

Sunday, April 13, 2003 10:50 PM

I received a letter from my son on Thursday, a short one, but happy. Said he is fine, in Iraq and very busy, said it's not for everyone but he likes it. Told me he had a good platoon. I still worry but it looks like things have really calmed down. Maybe it's almost over. I am so happy they found those POWs. This has been the most traumatic thing I have ever gone through. I am glued to that TV. . . . I have written to him and told him they are all very famous here. . . . Maybe I will get lucky and get a phone call from my son.

Sheila Malamut

27

Attacks Riddle Afghanistan, Including Shootings and Explosions

April 16, 2003

John e-mails a snippet of writing. It makes my day. I'm so relieved that I can still discern his writer's voice in spite of everything.

Driving in country is like riding a roller coaster without the assurance that millions before you have tried it and survived. Camels driven by their owners across the border and back again year after year from the beginning of time stand grazing on the side of the road. Dust billows across the horizon and the road, which is one of just a handful that anyone could describe as paved.

Dirt tracks extend left and right into the distance, up hills and off into the mountains, ending somewhere in the 14th century. But on this road jinga trucks roll into the future, decorated in outlandish colors and images of eyes, chains hanging from the undercarriage "jinga jangling" up and down this dusty track carrying a country's future with them.

April 17, 2003

I fall asleep in front of the TV. My father taps me on my shoulder. He is smiling. Then Dad fades away. I wake.

Al Qaeda has offered prize money for dead Americans. The Taliban is in Pakistan and attacking over the border. Why did I see my father? Has Dad come to lead John safely home? Which home?

My niece Beth—fifteen, kind, smart, pretty—is visiting from England. Genie and I took Beth to *Anger Management,* starring Adam Sandler. She enjoyed it. I did, too, mainly because I remember how much John liked *Happy Gilmore* when he was a teenager. John is in the desert looking for killers and I'm reduced to watching a dumb movie because it's a way to feel a little closer to John's youth. I'm not alone in my nostalgic craving for simpler days. Genie put it this way in a note to her sisters Pam and Molly:

With John so far away, I've worked out ways to give his shadow substance, enhance the bits of him I do have. I leave his old high school sports equipment by the back door. There are always lots of photos of him around the house. I reread some of his favorite books, The Hitchhiker's Guide to the Galaxy, *books about Thermopylae, King Xerxes, and the Greek wars, and* A Farewell to Arms. *I clean his room, but not too much; it was none too clean before the Marines and I want things as they were! I call Jessa a lot. Francis is an excellent listener too.*

I watch John's favorite movies, especially A Fish Called Wanda *and* Midnight Run, *but not the scary ones, not* Alien *or* Aliens. *I don't need to be made any more anxious than I am. I look at the old "Calvin and Hobbes" comic books John and I both love. (They are the new ones Frank bought him to replace the books he threw away years ago in a no-homework-no-fun crackdown!) I identify with the Mom Lady and John is Spaceman Spiff.*

Frank and I examine every piece of "John lore" together that we can recall; it helps to remember. One recurring story: John was ten and I was washing dishes after dinner one evening, my back turned to the kitchen; John crept up behind me and hissed softly on the back of my neck, his mouth half an inch away, sounding like the Alien in Aliens we had just watched in the movie! In an unthinking reflex I spun around fast and clipped him a good one on the side of his skull with my hand, the one that has that heavy ring on it. Stunned and hurt, he crumbled to the floor, rubbing the bump on his head. He couldn't believe I had done that. I wasn't about to apologize after he deliberately scared me out of my mind! John still brings this incident up as evidence of my "hard-hearted ways" and we've laughed about it many times. "Gotta watch out for her! She's tough!" John will say to friends.

I pray for John as I go through the day. I keep to my routine; keep the house in order, get my office work done, do some sewing, take walks with Frank, visit with family and friends—try to be busy. And sometimes I'm even sorry I bonked John on the head. . . .

Thursday, April 17, 2003 10:04 PM

I have served for 28 years in an agency of the Federal Government, and have lived overseas for several years representing this country. My agency has lost colleagues in the service of this great land, so I am keenly aware that even though I may not carry a rifle, our work has not been without risks. My husband served in Vietnam at the age of 17, not even able to vote in the country he served, wounded three times (the third almost killed him). . . .

I am often disheartened at the frightening ignorance and lack of awareness of the world in general that I see displayed by so many of my countrymen. I suppose that this sense of discouragement is heightened more because, in my profession, I can't avoid being informed of events taking place all over the world, the knowledge of threats to our security that few are privy to. At times, I wonder how we even survive. . . .

I am heartened to know that young men such as John have thought about something greater than themselves and have made the courageous step to serve this country. . . .

My heart has been a bit lighter and at peace knowing someone like John is out there, "watching our backs." I pray each day for the safety of those brave souls "just doing their job."

Sincerely,

Jeanne T.

April 18, 2003

3:44 AM. I wake bathed in the moonlight pouring through our skylights. Did this moon provide light for a terrorist as he wired an IED to kill John? Will they miss again? I find myself thinking about my mother.

Mom [Edith Schaeffer, eighty-eight years old and suffering from several small strokes and macular degeneration, lives in Switzerland with my sisters Priscilla and Debbie. —FS] does not sleep well. She repeats herself, forgets what happened yesterday but can still remember events from years ago. Last week when I called her, Mom said, "I'm awake a lot. I spend the night praying for John, for an angel to go in front of him, two more to walk on each side, and one to walk behind. I pray they will stop those bullets."

Strange that I've had so many battles with Mom, but now that it comes right down to it, knowing she's praying is such a source of comfort. Our fights over theology, my novels, and our diverging life paths mean little in the face of John going to war.

"Noni," as Mom's many grandchildren and great grandchildren call her, is visiting Jessica in Finland for a few days. It's the first time Amanda and Ben have seen Noni in their home. It may be the last. It's getting hard for her to travel. Last night I called Jessica and talked to Mom. She said she was having a good time.

"Mom, thank you for praying for John when you wake up in the night," I said.

"I forget a lot, but I *never* forget *that!*"

"Fight for my boy, Mom!" I blurted.

"I do."

Tuesday, April 15, 2003 5:04 AM

Papa, Noni is sleeping on the couch. She is all curled up with pillows. I was reading *Pride and Prejudice* to her and she conked out. I flew down to Helsinki yesterday to get her. All went well. She seems happy and relaxed, if tired. . . .

Well, you were on *Oprah!* OK, you have arrived at the heights! Even my friends here in Finland watch *Oprah.* What was it like? How did it go? How was she to work with? . . .

Noni made us all laugh coming up with excuses for not taking her medicine ("It's so much better for you if you skip a day or two!") and making up little songs about whatever she was doing that day. One time she made a song about her handbag and the only thing she could come up with for a rhyme was "I'm an old hag!"

Noni would often chirp old hymns or children's songs to herself quietly. Then she would ask the same question she just asked a minute before, equally content with any answer you felt like giving her at the moment. One night I put on Frank Sinatra for her and we danced to her favorite tunes. Noni loves to dance and it was heart-stopping to watch her try and do it alone, as she can't really see. . . . So I would dance with her, holding her up, and she would screw up all her strength to kick her leg or twist around and then be delighted. . . .

The kids aren't used to old women who joke and laugh and dance. I think she was very touched when they were so sad at her leaving. When I said she would only be with us a few more days both of them burst into tears.

Noni mentioned several times what a nice time you and she had had in NY together. So that has stuck with her. Noni remembered a lot about the trip, where you ate and what you did. It must have been important to her because she forgets most things. So you can take comfort in that.

I love you lots and am proud of you.

Jessica

28

Friday, April 18, 2003 11:49 PM

Help! We knew something was up. After his platoon's initial mission to the Iraqi oil platforms in the gulf Billy was calling us fairly regularly (once a week or so) and his girlfriend about every other day. . . . A week went by and Cyndi and I started wondering. . . . Then we knew that First Fast 3rd were most likely out and about again.

Details are always sketchy, but if you remember the Hornet aircraft that went down in Kabala, they were sent there shortly after that happened and were at the scene for a week. Billy said it was "very interesting" what they had to do but could say no more! These Special Forces . . . I swear! You can't read anything or see anything in the media about them!

. . .

Also I have tired of my American & Marine flags hanging off the front porch and just received the 20-ft. flagpole I ordered and will be raising it up tomorrow after the cement for the pole sleeve dries. I've got the underground wiring done for the night spotlight and all is "good to go. . . ."

Alan D. Ross

April 19, 2003

6:05 PM. I turn on the TV—professional bull-riding. I'm about to turn it off, but the announcer is talking about his son-in-law who is in the Marines. I watch.

Saturday, April 19, 2003 8:07 AM
From: Frank Schaeffer
To: Frank Gruber
  Dear Frank:
  What about encouraging your son, Henry, to enlist in a few years? There will be plenty to do! Looks as if we're in for a hundred years' war of religion however you slice it and whatever President Bush says about all of us worshipping the same god. And we had better hope the West wins.
  Good parents—and you and Janet are terrific parents—gently nudge their children in certain directions. I'll bet you've actively encouraged Henry to play an instrument, and to study. Why not plant the seed that military service would be good?
  What has surprised me is that having been so ambivalent about John joining the Marines, I feel sorry for his contemporaries who are missing the experience, even knowing how scared I am now that John is deployed.
  I don't mean I was ever anti-military, but I'm now pro-service in the same way as I'm pro-reading and pro-classical music and pro-jazz and pro-the Metropolitan Museum of Art.
  Maybe the USMC would be too much for everyone, though Henry looks fit to me! But I can't picture the kid who would not benefit from a few years of some sort of national service. This has less to do with patriotism than with character formation and developing a level playing field amongst all classes of persons and a sense of national community, otherwise known as fairness.
  What about all those rich kids cruising around Santa

Monica in fifty-thousand-dollar help-the-Saudis-kill-us-all-5-miles-to-the-gallon SUVs they got for their sixteenth birthday? Don't you think it would be good for them (and for our democracy), if they had to share a barracks room with a poor kid from Newark for a few years while embracing a purpose that transcends class, money, race, privilege, SAT scores, and religion? What about all these kids joining gangs up the street from you in Venice? Don't you think boot camp discipline and a chance to advance in a meritocracy would be good for them? And what about all those me-myself-and-I-self-esteem-for-no-reason middle-class lumps boozing it up in college?

Why should a few volunteers do all the heavy lifting? Last time I checked you didn't think only one class of Americans should pay taxes.

Best,

Frank

From: Frank Gruber
To: Frank Schaeffer
Saturday, April 19, 2003 6:27 PM

Hey, I thought that I *was* giving Henry the military option by suggesting he read *Keeping Faith!* So give me a break. Henry has plenty of military history on his shelf. Yes, we encourage him to read and to play an instrument—but he's going to decide what books he wants to read and what music he wants to play.

It's hard for me to prove this to you, but I have always been in favor of the draft. I had a 2-S (student) deferment back in 1970, but that was legitimate, and if the draft had still been in operation when I graduated in 1974, the military would have been happy to get a college graduate. Hey, where were you! Frank

29

AFGHANISTAN PRESSES PAKISTAN TO STOP CROSS-BORDER ATTACKS

Saturday, April 19, 2003 1:59 PM

My son Benedict is a lance corporal with the 2d Light Armor Reconnaissance. Unfortunately for Benedict, he was injured in training some months ago. After months of sucking it up in true Marine fashion, he saw a physician when he was home for Christmas. The upshot was that on March 19th, the day it all hit the fan, he was in surgery.

His back has been repaired, but it will never be 100% right again. He leaves for Lejeune tomorrow after 30 days of medical leave. I don't know what the USMC will decide about his fitness for service. Perhaps he'll go in the second wave of Marines to relieve those who've been there since January. He simply cannot talk about Iraq, or his colleagues who are there. His eyes fill with tears, and he changes the subject. He did everything he could to be deployed, but the doctors wouldn't fall in with his plans. . . .

Semper Fi,
Gretchen Brown

———————————

April 21, 2003

At church yesterday everyone said they are praying for John. Someone said, wanting to comfort me, "But the war is almost over, he'll be fine now." I'm not comforted! It's no relief that the war in Iraq is winding down. The clash of cultures will continue. Our young men and women will still be getting killed. Anyway, John is in Afghanistan, which I'm not mentioning to anyone yet, except to a few very close friends. Maybe I'm being paranoid, but I don't want to make him more of a target than he already is. I guess I've read one WWII account too many and those old phrases like "loose lips sink ships" stuck with me.

From: Frank Schaeffer
To: Frank Gruber
Monday, April 21, 2003 12:21 PM
    Dear Frank:
    I have to say that sometimes what we are doing in the Middle East seems futile. Already Al Qaeda and the Taliban are reestablishing themselves in Pakistan, where they are being hidden by the authorities sympathetic to their cause. The USA has no attention span and I worry that, sooner or later, we'll leave and the tide will come back in and it will be as if we've never been there. I just don't think our present political class, with the exception of John McCain, are cut out to be real leaders. We are soft!
    What is John risking his life for? I really wonder about the wisdom of fighting implacable enemies while observing all these multilateral "nation building" niceties.
    The memory we have of nation-building in Germany and Japan is no model at all. They weren't in the grip of Islamism, for one thing. And the post-sixties politically correct notion that we

have to respect the culture of our enemies means that we can never do in Afghanistan or Iraq what we did in Germany.

What would Germany be like today if we had "respected" the Nazi party and left it intact and worked with the more "moderate" Nazi elements? In Japan we invaded and told them that their emperor was no longer a god. We attacked and reformed a fascist religious/warrior culture by force. Now our policy is a combination of the worst of everything: "Regime change" combined with a soft over-solicitous respect for Islamism that is the natural enemy of freedom, women, democracy, and human rights.

Does that mean I think we should have done nothing after 9/11? No! And I'm glad we're knocking off Saddam! But I have no illusions that any of this, our invasions of Afghanistan and Iraq and my son's sacrifice is anything more than a holding action. We've been in Afghanistan and Iraq only a few months and already everyone wants to know if we're done yet and what our "exit strategy" will be! We have the weapons but do we have the will? Where is Winston Churchill when you need him?

Best,

Frank

From: Frank Gruber
To: Frank Schaeffer
Monday, April 21, 2003 7:03 PM

Don't worry about John. Not because there's nothing to worry about, but because he's doing good work and he's well trained. If I tell you there is hope of reforming the Islamic world, you'll just say I'm smoking some PC hallucinogen, but the bad guys John is after—and it's sure worth trying to catch them—are desperately bad precisely because they are scared of what America and the West are selling. I'm not being respectful of their culture, just respectful of what I believe are universal human desires (universal in the general sense, not with respect to every individual psychotic) for peace and prosperity for our children. Look what's happened in Iran—consistently 70–80 percent of the people vote for the good guys. So cheer up.

Frank

30

Monday, April 21, 2003 1:32 PM

I recently overheard a news commentator remark on how "low" the number of coalition casualties are in Iraq. I was watching the news with my son and pointed out that it may be a COMPARATIVELY low number but to the families of the service men and women lost it's EVERYTHING.

Kathleen M. Chambers

Monday, April 21, 2003 3:40 PM

What really amazes me is how our young adults have a more developed sense of patriotism and love of country than our generation of Baby Boomers. The young men and women fighting this war are mostly in their late teens and early twenties . . . just babies really. And the middle-aged adults of this country who comprise the Baby Boomers can't seem to shake the memories of our own youth and we are perpetually fighting against our parents, the government of Richard Nixon, and the legacy of Vietnam. The only problem with this is that our kids are viewing the world with more mature eyes than many of our cohorts.

Sue Jacobse

April 22, 2003

A wrong number at 4:30 AM is no longer just a wrong number. It's a heart-stopping event. I'm awake now! Yesterday afternoon I sent John a palm cross from our Palm Sunday service. John fills the house with his absence. He is a greater presence than when he lived in his room, ate breakfast every day, went off to school, played in the garden.

I keep looking at the various pictures of John, tucked into frames of paintings, on the stair walls. I touch them when I pass, try to revive the memories that now seem to be someone else's story. I can't feel the memories. The day-to-day intensity of missing John is burning them up, as if my brain just doesn't have room for both accurate memory and my experience of loss.

Spring is here. I planted four rose bushes yesterday but didn't take much pleasure in doing so. If something was not part of John's growing up, then what use is it? I know this is nuts. But now I understand why some old people live in tumbledown houses and don't change or fix anything. Why drive memory further into oblivion? Genie deals in her own way with keeping John's memory green.

I try not to think too much about how long it is between John's phone calls. If it gets too long, the anxiety level goes up and my life gets grim. I know I'm fortunate and blessed but between calls I just get dismal.

I sense the effect John's absence has on my daily routine by the enormous jolt I get when I pick up the phone and hear his calm voice say, "Hey, Mama." My whole being skips as if I've just been hit by a surge of electricity.

"Hey!" I say.

"What's up? How have you been?" asks John.

"We're fine, we're missing you! What have you been up to?"

"Oh, nothing much, I'm doing okay."

"That's great. . . ."

And then I scramble to recall bits and pieces of family news, trying to sense a connection, keep him close and tied to us even if I don't have much of importance to tell him. I try to discern by his tone and phrasing how he really is. He's always sounding tired, that's for sure, sometimes not too happy, sometimes distracted, mostly on cruise control. He's gotten so serious.

When I talk to him, I don't tell him things that might upset or discourage him. I make it clear we are coping and all is well. I sound cheerful about everything no matter how I'm feeling.

I know there is a chasm between us. I want to learn how wide it is. The best way to judge is by humor; give him a reference or a line that, in ordinary times, he would naturally supply the punch line to with a smile. If he can sense the humor in something I say, if he's relaxed enough to joke a little, then I can relax too, and it's an easier conversation. The ten minutes flies by too fast.

Once during the first weeks of boot camp, when we weren't getting much information from John because he was too disoriented (but I didn't know that), I sent him a multiple-choice letter. I meant it to be funny. In it I pretended I had misunderstood where he was, that I thought he was in Paris, France, instead of on Parris Island. I wrote such stupid stuff, asking about language differences, types of foods, room decor, pretending his DI was the tour guide, as if he were on vacation in France. I gave him various options as possible answers, all of them inane.

Ordinarily John would have gotten it and added a few choice items of his own. But when he returned the letter, I could tell from his responses (or lack thereof) how very stressed and out of it he was. He didn't even get the Paris/Parris pun. And John always gets everything. And that's when I knew how tough his life had gotten.

Attacks in Afghanistan

The New York Times, Tuesday, April 22, 2003
Gunmen fired on Bagram Air Base, the main American base in Afghanistan, on two occasions over the weekend, and one American soldier was wounded in a separate incident, an Army spokesman said. The shootings were among several attacks on coalition forces across Afghanistan by remnants of the ousted Taliban government and its allies. . . .
A Special Forces soldier was treated in Orgun, 110 miles south of Kabul, for a gunshot wound to the thigh, said spokesman Lt. Col. Doug Leforge. He did not say how the soldier was wounded.

From: Frank Schaeffer
To: John Schaeffer
Tuesday, April 22, 2003 8:24 AM
Subject: Are you okay?
I read in the *Times* that there were attacks on your base this weekend, also that a Special Forces soldier got wounded in another attack. Anything you want to tell me? Has any mail arrived?
Love
Dad

———————

3:35 PM. John called!
"I hear they were shooting at you guys this weekend," I said as nonchalantly as I could.
"Did they report that in the *Times?*" John asked, chuckling.
"Yes."
"They shoot at us all the time. The paper just happened to report

it this time. Don't worry, their aim isn't very good—and anyway, a lot of the time they're shooting at each other."

"Okay," I answered.

"They never clean their guns or sight in. So don't worry."

"Okay."

"Hey, Dad, the Italians really know how to go into the field!"

"What?"

"I went on a trip yesterday. We choppered to someplace I can't tell you about. Anyway, we were with these Italian Army guys."

"What were they doing there?"

"Oh, you know, just a meeting," John said, and laughed.

"Okay."

"Well, they were out there and they were cooking up pasta with porcini mushrooms! We had white wine to drink! I mean they brought it—chilled! You would've loved it!"

I had to laugh.

"Dad, I'm having such a terrific time."

"Great."

"And don't worry."

"Okay."

"I had a good day today. We're getting some really good things done."

"Any you can tell me about?"

"Nope."

"Did any of the mail arrive yet?"

"No, but it takes two to five weeks, so don't worry. I'm sending you a camera with some pictures."

The conversations with John are great but frustrating. Aware that the calls are short, I don't engage him in a real conversation, and I know I've done no more than scratch the surface, but I want to hear every last drop of news.

I long to learn how he's coping. Is he becoming a better or worse person, being hardened or made kinder? Is he surviving spiritually, emotionally? Has he killed people? Is he praying? Will he come home the son I've known? Is his cheerfulness on the phone as insincere as mine? Are we each trying to spare the other worry?

I comfort myself that the two pieces of his writing he sent still sound like him.

I called Jessica and told her John's news. We laughed about the Italians and the wine. "He's living large," she said.

After we talked all about John, Jessica asked, "What was Oprah like?"

"She was nice," I said. "But going on the show was really something."

"How?"

"When John and I went on *Nightline*, we just rolled in and sat in a little room, said hi to Ted Koppel, then went on."

"Right."

"With Oprah it's big-time. They put the guests through a metal detector, take away your cell phone, and won't let you carry your briefcase into the studio. Then you wait in a room, never meet Oprah till you're on the set. When she comes in it's like the queen of England's arrived."

"But what's *she* like?"

"Seems very nice but I only talked to her for about five seconds. She glanced down at the card and suddenly said, 'Are you the same Frank Schaeffer who wrote *Portofino*?' I said yes, and my heart skipped a beat. And then she said she read it while actually *in* Portofino and liked it!"

"The town or your novel?" Jessica said with a laugh.

"Yeah, yeah. You know what I mean! But *she didn't say it on the air!*"

"Poor Papa." Jessica laughed again.

"She started to say more, and then stopped when the commercial break ended. She started a new sentence: 'I liked your novel *Portofino*. . . .' Then we were back and she turned to the camera and said, 'We're back.' If you watch the tape when they cut from the commercial you can hear her talking to me as she turns back to the camera. You catch *ino*."

"Ino?"

"Half of Porto*fino*. *Ino!* See? Isn't that typical! I get HALF my novel's title on *Oprah! Just half!* '. . . *ino*. We're back.' "

Jessica was still laughing.

"You should've thrown yourself at her feet and begged, *'Please say that again on the air!'* "

"I seriously considered it."

31

April 23, 2003

2:45 AM. I'm in some sort of confused war zone preparing for battle. John is there. I'm having trouble sighting in an old rifle. I want to fire a practice shot. I ask John to help me sight in. By a mistake I fire the rifle. It takes a chunk of concrete out of a wall. The bullet ricochets around us.

April 24, 2003

John talked to Genie. She was pleased. John sounded happy, fulfilled, and content. "The happiest he's sounded in years," said Genie. John said they had a "really good couple of days," so he had been working double shifts. He said that as a result, "Everyone is coming to us now." He told Genie about wearing his bulletproof vest when he "goes to town"—Kabul—and carrying his sidearm.

Genie begged him to be careful. He said he was and that "ninety-five percent of the people like us, and the five percent that don't, can't shoot straight. . . ."

I worry about the five percent being better shots than John credits them for. Today in the *Times* they said more Afghan government officials and soldiers were killed by an IED.

April 25, 2003. Holy Friday

We are in Orthodox Easter Holy Week, a week later than the Catholic-Protestant Holy Week this year. Each night we have a service. Each night I light my candle for Genie, Jessica, Francis, and the grandchildren, and another one for John.

To celebrate our Orthodox Easter we'll roast a whole lamb on a spit set up in our garden. We've been doing this for thirteen years, since we converted. Theology aside, I'll take a spit-roasted, charcoal-grilled, oregano, lemon juice, and olive oil–basted lamb any day over lime Jell-O and honey-baked ham: evangelical Protestant Easter food!

I need to go to Home Depot and buy a few things, clamps to hold the lamb, a long pole for a spit. Home Depot takes good care of the families of their military reservists, so I make a point of shopping there.

I'll call Jimmy Andriotakis to see if he still has the rig we used at his place a few years ago. There is a photo in our kitchen of John as a teenager, standing next to Jimmy, with a lamb carcass over his shoulders. They are both laughing. I wonder if John will remember that it's Orthodox Easter.

John and Jimmy loved to pick up the whole lamb from the supermarket after Jimmy's mother, Stella, or Genie special-ordered it. John always made sure to stick it on the checkout conveyor belt headfirst, for the full "What-*is*-that? shriek effect," as he called it. It was never a good Easter unless John could get one of the checkout girls to scream. After fasting from meat for forty days, that lamb loomed large!

ROADSIDE BOMB KILLED FOUR AFGHAN WORKERS

AMERICANS ATTACKED

As of yesterday, John was fine. One other news item: an Italian was killed. I wonder if he is one of the soldiers who gave John a glass of wine.

12:52 PM. I jump in my ancient rusting truck to go buy a picnic table. We want it for the roast lamb dinner on Sunday. I turn on the radio. "Today an American soldier was killed and five wounded when a patrol in southern Afghanistan was attacked."

I have to stop the truck and sit in the driveway. One killed, five injured. My hands are shaking. I feel as if I have just had an icicle shoved up my rectum.

6:21 PM. I've been trying to get more news but can't find anything. Surely by now they'd be here if it was John. This is Good Friday: Christ crucified. I think enough time has passed so they would be here by now if it was John. Someone else is getting the news of a beloved child taken.

From: Frank Gruber
To: Frank Schaeffer
Saturday, April 26, 2003 4:47 PM
Without being melodramatic, when I heard that Americans had been killed in Afghanistan, my heart jumped into my throat. How selfish we get—I know John, so I was relieved when the dead were described as "soldiers," not Marines. I was still nervous.
Frank

John sends his shortest e-mail ever, with copies to his friends. In fact there is no message, just a "subject line." I guess given the news John wants us all to know he's okay.

From: John Schaeffer
To: Everyone
Friday, April 25, 2003 7:57 PM
Subject: Hey, everyone!

32

IN AFGHANISTAN VIOLENCE STALLS RENEWAL EFFORT

April 26, 2003

Last night at the Good Friday service, Father Kerry was walking through the crowded church sprinkling us all with Holy Water. He used something that looked like a silver baby's rattle, only with holes in it so the droplets sprayed out as he flicked it. He hesitated as he passed Genie and me and, with a nod and smile, gave us an extra-big sprinkle. I knew the extra shot was for John, and received the droplets for him. I'm grateful almost out of proportion to Father Kerry for his kindness.

Ever since my *Washington Post* op-ed re some Orthodox leaders signing that peace letter, Father Kerry has been very tender to Genie and me, as if he wants to make sure we know he is supporting John and us in every way. I take him aside after the service and explain to him that my argument is not with our local church, him, or Orthodoxy, but only with some people within the Church who signed on to a very ill-conceived document. He gives me a hug and reminds me he is praying for John. He is a real priest, a true father.

After the service, everyone crowded around asking about John. Another day ends with no van coming down my drive, no uniformed personnel bringing bad news. Tomorrow is Holy Saturday, then the lamb roast on Pascha [Easter] Sunday, the most joyful day in the Greek Orthodox calendar. John loved sitting by the lamb and slowly turning the spit, the sips of ouzo, the lemon-rice-lamb soup that Stella always brought, Jimmy Andriotakis's joking about those checkout girls. . . .

The Sunday *Times* has more details of the most recent killing.

. . .

The war [in Afghanistan] has not ended—as shown by an attack today that killed two American soldiers and by a planned visit on Sunday from Defense Secretary Donald H. Rumsfeld. Nearly every day, there are killings, explosions, shootings and targeted attacks on foreign aid workers, Afghan officials, and American forces, as well as continuing feuding between warlords in the regions. . . .

The attack today, which killed an American soldier near a Special Forces base close to Shkin in eastern Afghanistan, was particularly brazen. About 20 rebels opened fire on a platoon of American and Afghan soldiers in broad daylight, wounding at least six other soldiers before retreating across the border to Pakistan, as many attackers have in recent weeks.

A second American soldier later died of wounds from the battle. . . . American soldiers at their headquarters at Bagram Air Base, near Kabul, share many of the apprehensions of the Afghan public—despite their public, official optimism on their ability to secure both Afghanistan and Iraq. . . .

April 28, 2003

There was a large picture in the paper of six soldiers carrying a flag-draped coffin with the caption FALLEN SOLDIER IN AFGHANISTAN. In the background were tall mountains that reminded me of the Swiss Alps. Standing nearby were a group of soldiers, watching. I blink back tears and peer at the blurred faces to see if one is John.

---

10 PM. I was jolted awake by the phone. It was John! The connection was not good. I had to shout. John had remembered it was Orthodox Easter and gave the appropriate greeting in Greek.

"*Christos Anesti*!" shouted John. "Christ is risen."

"*Alithos Anesti*!" I yelled back. "Truly he is risen."

"Hey, Pop."

"Hey, big guy. I saw a picture in the paper of soldiers carrying the coffin of one of our guys."

"I was standing there watching as the coffins were loaded."

"Are you okay?"

"Yes."

"We thought about you all Easter. Everybody asked after you."

"Good."

"How are you?"

"Very busy. There's a lot going on."

I began to scribble notes.

"The mail arrived, hit all at once. . . . Delivery is about twice a week. . . ."

"What about the pictures?" I asked.

"The next disposable camera is on the way home. . . ."

"You sound good."

"Rounding the home stretch on a twelve-hour shift. . . . As my OIC [officer in charge] says, 'We can sleep in July. . . .' Home in the middle of June or July. . . . Difficult for us when the guys got killed. . . . Nothing we could do. . . . Part of our job is to help keep them safe. . . . When the 82nd Airborne gets pissed, they roll into town to ask questions or shoot you. . . . It was their guys killed. . . . We felt bad. . . . We try and find out what is needed to keep our guys safe.

. . . Dad, we couldn't keep them safe. . . . Some of the pictures I've sent were taken of me walking around Kabul looking unusually heavy because of the bulletproof vest under my civvy clothes and a bulge from the sidearm. . . . Not much of a question what I'm carrying. . . . Get copies of my pictures for everybody. . . . Cold at night. . . . Really boiling in our tent in the day. . . . Big tent, sun beats down. . . . Oh, I gotta go. Love you, Dad!"

"Watch your back, John."

"I'll do that. . . ."

"I love you, John."

33

April 28, 2003 (continued)

I can't sleep. I check my e-mails. John has sent a poem.

standing at attention
humvee rolls slowly by
salute brought up and held
death carried
flags draped
two men
heart wrenching sacrifice

34

April 29, 2003

I called our nearby neighbors [they live in the next town] Cathy and Danny Boucher. I got their answering machine. Their oldest son, Lieutenant Max Boucher, is at Camp Lejeune. Lance Corporal Asher, their youngest, is deployed to Iraq with the 1st Marine Division. Danny's outgoing message was:

"Hello, this is Cathy and Danny. And, Ash, if you call again, we got the message you left. We're so proud of you and grateful for what you're doing for our country. Call back if you can. And tell the other troops we're proud of you all. We love you."

Danny's voice had that thick throaty sound mine gets these days when I talk about my Marine. It must have killed Danny to miss his son's call from Iraq. There was so much longing in his voice. The infantry guys don't get to call nearly as often as John does. Danny hasn't heard from Ash for over a month. I know we are extremely fortunate to hear from John more often.

From: Frank Schaeffer
To: Frank Gruber
Tuesday, April 29, 2003 3:18 AM
    2:40 AM. Awake again! Genie and I are both feeling

depressed. The separation seems really long. The pictures he sent made it worse, not better, though we were delighted to see them. Afghanistan looks so poor. I know he'll be feeling badly that he can't do more for the people. On the other hand, every time we talk to him he has a very steely resolve when it comes to work.

I'll give you a little mental exercise. My son is at war watching your back. You are my best friend. Okay? So put an American flag on your door and maybe even a lapel pin of a flag on your shirt.

Will you do this, Frank? If not, why not? I'll bet you have a million arguments why it would just not be "appropriate" for you to be mistaken as a supporter of our military. How about just a yellow ribbon if you can't manage a flag?

Best,

Frank

From: Frank Gruber
To: Frank Schaeffer
Tuesday, April 29, 2003 5:29 PM

You probe deep with the question about whether I would tie a yellow ribbon on a tree or fly a flag in the front yard or wear a flag lapel pin. This one is tough. You're right, I don't wear a flag pin and we've never flown a flag in front of the house. There's never been much discussion about this, although after 9/11 I thought about it and it would have been easy to get a flag.

As you know from what I wrote in my column, I got fairly emotional about America after that. I also wrote about singing "The Star-Spangled Banner" in public, at Henry's Little League and at the opera and the Philharmonic. The fact is, I'm unhappy about what's happened with the flag, as growing up we always flew it at home on Memorial Day and July 4th, etc., but I can't ignore the fact that these symbols that should belong neutrally to everyone have been taken over by the right, and we on the left allowed this to happen.

I remember in the 1988 campaign when Bush appeared at the flag factory in New Jersey. But maybe I'm chicken about this. In part, chicken that people will mistake me for a right-winger, but also too scared as a left-winger to take these symbols back. It looked like this would happen after 9/11, but as of this moment, again, flags and yellow ribbons have become exclusionary rather than inclusionary symbols.

But you're right—it's just as much my fault—as a leftie—that this has happened as it is the right wing's fault, because people like me on the left let it happen. If we had all responded to Bush's trip to the flag factory by going out, all of us on the left, and buying flags, and putting them in our yards, maybe then the flag would not have become politicized then, and if we had all done the same after 9/11, maybe it wouldn't be that way now.

Everyone gets the worse for it when political decisions become mixed up with patriotism. It's terrible that anyone should be self-conscious about waving the flag, but it's true, we are—not only people on the left, but also people on the right who use it for their own purposes. Both sides are self-conscious about it. The only place that patriotic symbols seem completely neutral is at sporting events—when we sing the "SSB" at Dodger Stadium, or down at the Little League field, where there are no politics.

Frank

———————————

From: Frank Schaeffer
To: Frank Gruber
Tuesday, April 29, 2003 11:28 PM

You're so uptight about your left-wing "theology" that even putting up an American flag becomes a convoluted struggle!

You're just as much a fundamentalist about your secular leftist beliefs as my mom is about her Bible! This is what happens when a political ideology gets taken a little too seriously and, in fact, becomes a person's religion. Your "inclusiveness" is so rigid *it's* exclusionary!

You pay a price—the loss of common sense—by politicizing every issue to such an extent. I'll go further and say that in this day and age anyone that can even be identified as "of the left" or "of the right" is silly. Life is too big to speak to all issues with one consistent voice. Two words are missing from your political vocabulary: paradox and mystery. A seamless worldview is evidence of a limited imagination.

I don't think this issue of the flag is really political. I think it's an issue of class. For people like you, in the educated wealthy "Hollywood left," the flag is something you associate with the lower classes. Admit it! You are surrounded by a bunch of overpaid snobs! To them, construction workers and women with big hair fly flags. Flying the flag would embarrass you in the same way as having to put a little plastic gnome on your lawn would. Don't dignify your snobbery as political conviction.

Best,
Frank

35

April 29, 2003 (continued)

A poem e-mailed from John . . .

    dust blows and the wind kicks up cold
    bringing the smells of flatbread
    burning trash
    unwashed populace
    chicken street flows past Sammy's shop
    I sit on a folded three thousand dollar rug
    that anywhere in America
    would fetch twenty thousand dollars
    Sammy feeds me
    chicken and lamb with flatbread
    I am wearing body armor
    am armed with an m-4 and m-9 with over 150 flesh tearing
        rounds on my body
    despite these things I would be nowhere else than eating with
        Sammy
    hearing first about the Russians and then the Taliban
    from this man who survived both and sends his daughter to
        school now
    because he is finally allowed to

36

Saturday, May 03, 2003 12:40 PM
Subject: Re: "Ski" from Ft Huachuca
    Hello, Shaf's Dad:
    We're stationed out of the Medina Annex (part of Lackland
AFB) in San Antonio, TX . . . Ski is doing pretty well, he just
finished some sort of military communications course. (I've
enclosed some pictures from our wedding.) He really misses
his old buddy "Shaf" [John Schaeffer] from Ft. Huachuca,
and wanted me to have you pass on that message. . . . If
John's home around late July that would be nice, since Ski
is going to go back home to upstate NY and he really wants
John to visit.
    Rachel Ludwikowski

May 7, 2003

5:18 AM. I woke obsessing about John's poem. Now I'm worried
that he's wandering Kabul looking for some deal on a carpet to bring
me as a present! I worry that he'll get killed doing something unnec-
essary. No word since the poem.

May 9, 2003

2:49 AM. "Pick up the phone!" I said. Genie grabbed for the phone but no one was there. The ringing was just in a dream. I can't get back to sleep. Was it actually ringing? Two soldiers were killed in Baghdad yesterday: one by a sniper, the other on a bridge, shot point-blank by a man with a pistol. The war in Iraq is "over." So is the war in Afghanistan. Now American soldiers will be murdered one by one or in twos or threes.

May 10, 2003

7:00 PM. John called. I raced to the phone from the screened porch. Genie and I had just sat down to dinner.

"It's John," I shouted, "pick up!"

Genie dashed to her office. I took the call in the kitchen.

"Hey, Mama."

"How are you?" asked Genie.

"I guess the phones will be all tied up this weekend, so I wanted to call early and wish you a happy Mother's Day."

"How did you know it's Mother's Day?" Genie asked.

"Oh, things get around. So I wanted to call."

"Thank you," said Genie.

"That's great," I said. "How have you been?"

"Fine, except we're short, so I've been working sixteen-hour days, but it's great."

"So did you get the P. G. Wodehouse I sent?" I asked.

"Yes, but I didn't have time to read it yet."

"They sold four thousand six hundred of our books to the History Book Club," I said.

"Does that count toward the weekly sales total for the best seller list?" asked John.

I laughed.

"No, it's a special deal, but still great," I answered.

John was working a sixteen-hour day, remembering Mother's Day, and ready to discuss the best seller list! My spirits rose instantly.

"I sent three cameras off, or will when my NCOIC [non-commissioned officer in charge] remembers. He forgot to send the other camera. Well, now there's two more, so that makes three on the way."

"Great," said Genie. "I can't wait."

"Also, I'm putting some hand-carved chess pieces, a set, in for Francis's birthday, but don't forget the Scotch and diapers for him."

"We won't." I laughed again.

"I need some more money, a couple of hundred more. Just take it out of my bank account."

"Do you get to PT [physical training] with all the work you're doing?" asked Genie.

"Yes, once in a while our OIC takes over and says, 'Go take some time, PT or nap or whatever.' So he gives us time sometimes."

"What about the Italians?" asked Genie.

"I haven't seen them again," said John with a chuckle. "And I don't think they ever do PT!"

"Are you going out on any more missions?" I asked.

"I haven't for a few days, maybe next week we'll be out doing something."

"Great," I said, as my heart sank. "Do you still think you'll be home by the end of June?"

"Maybe I'll be home in time to come up and see Jessica while she's there. But don't tell her, in case it doesn't work out. I don't want to disappoint her again."

"Well, if you get back, we'll all do whatever we need to, to get you together with Jessa and the kids," said Genie.

"As soon as I'm home I'm taking some leave and will come right up. But it depends if they train the next guy in time to get out here. Right now we're short."

"Well, I hope you can be back in time," said Genie.

"I've been renovating the old shed into a guest room," I said. "It's my summer project. We'll put in a bed. When you're home you can stay there. It'll have its own entrance so you can come and go."

"Hey, I'll probably want to live there," said John.

"Sounds great," I said.

"It's going to be beautiful," said Genie.

"My call ends in about twenty seconds, so happy Mother's Day, Mom!"

"Thank you," said Genie. "We love you. We've been missing you. It happens at odd times. The other day I called Dad and got your voice; remember you did the message for him on his cell phone when you gave it to him for Christmas?"

"Right."

"Well," said Genie, with a catch in her voice, "hearing you suddenly, when I wasn't expecting it, really made me miss you."

The phone clicked off. Genie and I walked back to the deck and finished our dinner.

"Someday he'll have his own kids," I said.

"Then he'll know," Genie said as she sat down across from me on the deck.

It was a lovely evening and the marsh was greening up into its full spring glory. John seemed so far away.

From: Frank Schaeffer
To: Frank Gruber
Saturday, May 10, 2003 5:27 AM

Dear Frank: What you don't get is that to a soldier or a Marine's parent the flag isn't political. It's personal.

I've learned something from John, from the people he works with and from their families. Frank: There is an America that you seem to have no empathy for. That America rallies around our flag not because we are of the "right" or "left" but because we are first and foremost loyal to our families and to our military brotherhood.

Next time you see a tattered American flag fluttering off a highway overpass, don't think to yourself, "That was put there by a bunch of right-wingers." Rather know that it was put there by a father or mother or wife or husband or girlfriend of some soldier earning so little that his or her wife or husband and children are on food stamps while he or she is overseas sleeping on the ground. The soldier's family put that flag there because we love him. And we love the flag because our soldier (or Marine) is proving by his sacrifice that he loves us. The flag unites us.

That's why we put up the flag on our gate: it's a way to feel close to John while he's a world apart. It is a way to tell every person in the military family we are proud of them. It's not a "left wing" or "right wing" symbol, Frank; it's our family saying, "We love you" to John and to all our sons and daughters who wear the uniform.

Best,

Frank

37

It's a bright sunny Sunday morning. I was basking in the glow from John's call, *until* I read the Sunday *Times*.

> KABUL, Afghanistan. — Late Friday an American soldier was wounded and an Afghan soldier killed in an ambush. . . . The ambush was the latest in a series of attacks. . . . Although Defense Secretary Donald H. Rumsfeld announced the end of major combat operations during a visit to Afghanistan last week, attacks by Taliban or other rebels are occurring almost daily on American soldiers. . . .

May 13, 2003

Yesterday Genie packed a big box and sent it to John. She bought him a kids' badminton set and a toy horseshoe game, some balls you soak in water and throw water-fight style, and a lot of candy, dried fruit, and other treats. She also stuck in some more baby wipes and foot powder. John said he still had plenty of personal hygiene items but that anything he couldn't use he'd pass on to other Marines and soldiers.

"Attacks by Taliban or other rebels are occurring almost daily on American soldiers." I don't like the odds.

I dug a trench for the new foundation-footing for the shed-to-guest-room project. I mixed up and poured the concrete into molds, adding rebar. Each time I picked up and heaved a bag of ready-mix concrete, I thought about my Marines carrying their eighty pounds of equipment. I unloaded forty eighty-pound bags off the truck in three batches, mixing up the concrete in my wheelbarrow and shoveling it into the mold. I worked so hard, my hands are numb and I'm having trouble typing. In some strange way I'm trying to somehow share in John's struggles. I know this doesn't make sense.

Cathy and Danny Boucher came over last night. They just received a letter from Asher. He wrote that he fought his way into Baghdad and did a lot of shooting, and that the Marines saved all the candy that parents and friends sent, Skittles and M&M's and such, to give to Iraqi children. He said he was feeling weird at being "kissed by so many Iraqi men" who were happy about their liberation.

Later I asked Genie what she thought Ash would do once he gets back, how he'll feel. Genie knew what I was really asking and quietly replied: "Maybe John has shot someone too." She seemed neither happy nor sad, just resigned. I'm wondering if I'll dare ask that question when he comes home.

A compound in Saudi Arabia was attacked last night. Many are dead, many wounded. Americans were the targets. The Taliban killed six more Afghan soldiers.

May 14, 2003

8:36 PM. John called. I took notes for Jessica and Francis.

"I've been here a month and a half now but it feels like a day and a half. The children follow us and love Americans because we give them candy. Someone taught them a thumbs-up sign, so they do that—must have been the same person who taught them to shout 'Fuck Taliban!' "

"Do people hate you?" I asked.

"The farmers love us because they've had a drought for ten or twenty years or something and this year they've had more rain than since 1960."

"What?" I asked.

John chuckled.

"Some of these farmers aren't really very Muslim, more traditional superstitious pre-Islamic nomads; anyway, they think we changed their luck, so they love us. . . . I'm leaving on a mission in about two hours. . . . Don't worry; it's not too dangerous."

"How are your living conditions?" Genie asked.

"Fine, but you have to remember where you are. We have potable and nonpotable water; we can drink the potable but only shower or wash clothes in the nonpotable—not even shave in it, let alone brush our teeth."

"How about the other guys?" I asked. "Do you all get on?"

"Sure. I get on well with our guys; our NCOIC and our OIC are great guys. We have a new NCOIC coming out; he's a Marine I already know, so this will be very cool."

"And you're fine?" Genie asked.

"Sure, but I've got dust in some interesting places!" John laughed. "I'll be washing the sand off of everything I own for months after I get home. . . ."

Genie and I spent an hour rehashing the call, savoring and analyzing every word, the tone of John's voice—tired, calm, and happy—what was behind the words, how we felt about his mood, what we forgot to ask, how little he really tells us about what he's doing, if we believe his mood is as positive as he makes it sound. . . .

May 15, 2003

3:00 AM. The knowledge that John is out on a mission wakes me. I watch a replay of an interview of the Saudi Foreign Minister, Prince Bandar, by Dan Rather. The prince tells Rather that the Saudi government is doing all they can to help find and stop the "evil men" from doing more "evil things." He says Islam is a religion of "peace and science and tolerance." What peaceful, tolerant scientist wants to kill my son this morning?

It's time to take out the garbage. My *New York Times* is on the drive . . . waiting. I hope there is news about Afghanistan and I hope there is not.

Germany has just expelled a senior Saudi diplomat after the police linked him to raising funds for Al Qaeda.

5:00 AM. As I stepped into the kitchen the sweet narcissus scent was strong. I could smell the cluster of tall white flowers from across the room. I had picked them last night. I carried the garbage cans up to the road one at a time instead of putting them on the pickup truck. There is enough noise in the world and I want to deprive Prince Bandar and his peaceful, tolerant scientists of a cent or two.

From now on I'll always take the train whenever I can. I want to wipe that smarmy, arrogant grin off Bandar's face. The birds were singing, their voices echoed under the canopy of new leaves shimmering above me. Everything in the garden is lovely this morning—perfect, cool, and still.

May 16, 2003

Genie read me an article over breakfast.

Tickets, Lifestyle Guru? All Set
By Karen Robinovitz

When Denise Rich was planning a recent trip to Aspen, she meticulously packed her essentials—toiletries, ski gear, thermals, oh, and yoga instructor. That's right, yoga instructor. Ms. Rich, the songwriter and ex-wife of Marc Rich (the fugitive financier pardoned by Bill Clinton just before he left the presidency), takes her own personal guru when she hits the road.

It may seem like indulgence to the nth degree, but in some echelons of society, where a $1,000 handbag is considered a bargain and conversations about Iraq are conducted over dinner at Jean Georges, it is a necessity. In today's stressful times, there is a belief that a trusted expert, someone whose job is to keep you centered (or well fed or coifed or thin), offers solace and a sense of equanimity.

"Because the world is in such an upset and such turmoil, it's so important to come inside yourself with something like meditation, rather than focus on what is going on around you," Ms. Rich said just before the war in Iraq began. She said that she considered what she paid her guru, Jules Paxton, "a gift to myself." . . . "It's anxiety-provoking to watch the news or even read the paper," Ms. Rich said. "When I go to yoga and find a meditative state, I embrace calm and have more strength to deal with what's going on."

. . .

Todd Rome, the president of Bluestar Jets, a private jet company, said that he had seen this type of thing for ages, but he was seeing it now "on a whole new level."

"It's no longer just limited to nutritionists and trainers and such," he said. "People are flying with their hair and makeup artists and manicurists. We've had yoga teachers give people in-flight classes and we've had chefs traveling with our big honcho clients on our jets, feeding their employers Alaskan king crab and caviar. . . ."

Genie finishes reading. She laughs.

"Bring back the guillotine," I mutter.

Friday, May 16, 2003 1:22 AM

I have so many stories to tell you—most of which I can't tell over the Internet. I'm still in Iraq and for some reason someone has it in our command's mind that my unit needs to be here until the end of the war. However, my CO may send me back early because Peter is deploying again in December. Anyway, Peter is in Kuwait and should be home any day now. I'll try to send more pictures of our "honeymoon" in Iraq.

Love,

Jane Vizzi Blair

Friday, May 16, 2003 2:27 AM

From: John Schaeffer

Subj: News

Mom, Dad: In your paper tomorrow you'll read about some Marines shooting up some Afghan government soldiers. I don't think the *Times* will like it, but we have better information and our guys had their reasons.

J

May 21, 2003

A package arrived from John. He sent a birthday present for Francis and a letter for all of us, as well as a birthday present for Genie. There were also three disposable cameras. The pictures will be ready in an hour.

The letter tucked into the box was written over several weeks. It was mailed about two weeks ago, but the first pages are from just after John arrived in Afghanistan. A lot of it looks hastily written, sometimes in an almost illegible scribble. The box was full of grit and red dust; the letter is smudged with dusty fingerprints.

Hey folks,

How ya doin'? Life here is busy, just thought I'd drop you a line. Things are going fine. I'm working hard. Not that much sleep these days, I'm working nights mostly. I find that to be more interesting than days although I end up doing that too some days.

Bo says "hi." He's one of the guys I work with, nice. Probably the best guy we've got out here right now as far as the job goes. I'm gonna write in installments I think, less short letters. So for now, see ya.

Hey, I'm back, a few days later. It's mostly hot out here. There's an occasional breeze, which is nice, but with the breeze comes the dust. It's either heat or dust and sometimes both. What a wonderful place! Afghanistan is a country where every increasingly worthless inch has been coated with the blood of men from the Persians to Alexander to the British to the Americans.

Gotta go to work.

Went and saw some of the PUCs (Persons Under Custody) today. That's your average Al Qaeda/Taliban type, in case you're wondering. It was nice to know they'll never be free. I hope they keep them here forever. It'll be less than they deserve. I've seen some of the things they do.

Hey guys, I'm back. Bo's gone back to the US now. It's a few weeks after the last time I wrote but I might as well continue here. I apparently did not mail the cameras as I had thought. Chief was going to do it for me but we're so busy I guess he forgot. On the plus side now you get three cameras!

The presents:

Chess set is for Francis on his birthday, although this may arrive late, so I will remind you on the phone to get the Scotch and diapers and/or bedpan. The circular box is for Mom.

Have no fear, there are other things out here as presents for you all—no one will be left out, especially you, Jessa.

Love,

Your nutcase boy

At supper, rather, before supper, I bickered with Genie about the amount of flounder she bought. I'm hungry after working on the property all day, mowing then building. I'm in my jerk/chef, I'm-a-man-of-the-working-people, feed-me mode. I snap at her about buying "too little food." After supper I apologize. There was more than enough fish. Then we talk about the box from John and the pictures. Tonight's TV news: Marines in Kabul, guarding the U.S. embassy, shot and killed four Afghan government soldiers. It was a "misunderstanding," says a spokesman for the Afghan military. This must be the incident John referred to in his e-mail.

We got John's pictures back. The landscape is bleak! John looks as if he's on another planet! The homeland security alert is "orange" tonight. Where and when will we be attacked next? My contribution to the war effort is to bicker about flounder while John is living on MREs.

May 22, 2003

4:45 AM. It's a little muggy. One of the pictures John sent was of the wall in some sort of recreation room/bar in Kabul, which our men and women have dubbed the "Talibar." Our soldiers have scrawled all sorts of graffiti on the walls. John shot pictures. One Magic Marker contribution read as follows:

When you're wounded and left lying on Afghanistan's
  plains,
And the women come out to cut up what remains,
Just roll to your rifle and blow out your brains,
An' go to your gawd like a soldier.
—Rudyard Kipling

John grew up reading Kipling's stories of the "white man's burden" and Victorian outposts of empire. Maybe I'll reread my collection and find out where John goes next.

From: Frank Schaeffer
To: Frank Gruber
Thursday, May 22, 2003 4:40 AM
  Dear Frank:
  Last evening was intense. Looking at the pictures, one of how vulnerable our son appeared in his bulletproof vest and a second, taken by John, of another Marine asleep next to a machine gun poking out of a helicopter door (when they were

flying to some mission), combined with the heightened terror alerts here at home made everything feel so crazy and unstable. You may be an optimist but my mood is closer to the text of the book featured on the cover of last Sunday's *Times Book Review* section: *Our Final Hours!*

Best,

Frank

May 23, 2003

2:39 AM. I study the pictures John sent of himself standing, surrounded by Afghan children. The *New York Times* is printing the names of military personnel killed in Iraq in tiny boxes—name, date of death, and rank—sometimes with no news story about who they were or how they died. They report the deaths in headlines, but now that the sexy part of the war is over, *who* got killed is an afterthought.

A soldier who has sexually harassed a cadet at a military academy often rates more coverage than a soldier killed in the service of his or her country. If the publisher of the *Times* had a son or daughter serving, I'll bet the coverage would be different. How, I'm not sure, but different.

38

Friday, May 23, 2003 5:31 AM

Greetings from beautiful Beaufort, home of Parris Island and sand gnats! My Marine, Daniel, got to tour the ancient city of Babylon last weekend. I was so excited for him. He sent pictures of where his namesake, Daniel the prophet, was thrown into the lion's den. There is much prophecy in Scripture against this city, saying it will lay desolate. I was reminded of the truth of that when I saw the ruins. A once great city and people taken down by pride. . . .

So many Marines have come home. I'm anxiously waiting (as I'm sure you are) for my Marine to arrive, hopefully in June. I am thankful that we both can celebrate Memorial Day NOT having to visit our sons' graves. I will be going to our National Cemetery here in Beaufort to pay respects to fallen heroes.

Godspeed to you and John.

Chuck Beach

May 24, 2003

John e-mails a piece of writing.

Days in a desert seem to run headlong one into the other. Finding a separation between two or three requires a distinct event. This event is often hard to find when the look of every day is precisely the same. You can count on the fact that it will be hot, windy, dry. At night it will be a little cooler, a little less windy, and dry. It does not make for a very exciting existence.

Life on a military base can really compound this problem. Designed with routine in mind, the life of a base grinds by as one day seamlessly folds into the next. You are lucky to know what month it is or even what planet you are on.

None of this is to say that for some, life does not move incredibly fast, especially for those of us that actually have something to do, besides guarding the wire. Now, guarding the wire is an incredibly important task and the men doing that job ensure my safety, for which I am eternally grateful. But it does not exactly lend itself to great mental challenges; beyond counting the mines you can see from behind the wall, one more time.

For a minority of us the time flies at an incredible pace. Whether it is stress or interest in the work or merely a massive workload, time, for us of the lucky few with a challenging job, really hauls ass. . . .

AFGHANISTAN; FIVE ARE ARRESTED IN REPORTED PLAN TO SET OFF BOMB IN KANDAHAR

May 26, 2003. Memorial Day

4:40 AM. Genie and I were crawling on a steep slope above a cliff. I began to slip and fall and reached out to grasp the branches of a bush that came loose. The branch turned into a piece of cloth and I suddenly could see the end of the cloth as it slid through my wildly clutching hand. I was tumbling inexorably over the edge. I glanced down the cliff and saw nothing but jagged rocks at the bottom. I wanted to reach out and grab Genie to steady myself and realized I'd pull her down too. I woke up. I can't remember ever having so many clear and horrible dreams.

Last night on TV there was a Memorial Day story about a Navy corpsman who died trying to save a wounded Marine in Iraq. The corpsman was twenty-two. The President made a Memorial Day speech. He was on the verge of tears as he spoke of those killed.

39

May 27, 2003

A poem from John . . .

Chief Kerns, that mustached behemoth
dominating a room the way only a West Virginian can
tells me of hunting among mountains and hills
the time his sister shot him in the head
his children
girlfriends before his wife
his wife
his son, his daughter
he will go back to those hills and mountains
when he is done with the Navy, and the sea
and he will hunt, he says, and watch NASCAR
he will not have to miss any more races for war
and he is happy

40

May 28, 2003

"It's John!" yelled Genie.

I dashed inside, ditching work gloves and scattering dust, painfully aware that the seconds of the call were ticking away.

"Hi, John!" I panted.

"Hey, Dad," said John, sounding tired and a long way off.

"How have you been?"

"Fine."

"How are all those kids?"

"Fine. They love having their pictures taken."

"They looked great."

"They love us, when they're not trying to steal whatever is in our pockets!" John laughed.

"We read about the Marines shooting those guys at the U.S. embassy," said Genie.

"The *Times* quoted some Afghan who said it was a misunderstanding," I said.

"I've never heard the word 'misunderstanding' applied to pointing a machine gun at a Marine tower guard before. That's interesting. . . . Hey, I have some news. It looks as if I'll be getting out of here by around June twenty."

It took a moment for the news to sink in. I heard Genie gasp.

"Terrific!" I exclaimed.

"You might be home in time to see Jessica!" said Genie, in a voice well on the way to becoming a joyful shriek.

"Right, well, my replacement will come out, then I'll train him for a few days, then I'll take three days to a week to get back, depending on military flights out of Germany," said John nonchalantly.

I could tell John was excited but trying to act the cool, calm Marine.

"This is great!" I said.

After John's call, Genie and I were practically dancing around the house. We talked about how excited Jessica will be if she is able to see her little brother. It's been four years since we were all together.

"We don't want to disappoint her," said Genie. "Don't say a thing till we're certain."

Before he hung up, John mentioned that he had heard from his Marine buddy, Patrick, that something is wrong with our old Ford. The back wheels are locked up. I'll call my garage and ask Phil—whose brother is in the Marines and who, ever since he saw my USMC bumper sticker, has been giving me super service—what to do. Then I'll get in touch with Patrick and arrange to get it fixed before John gets home. I'm planning to go down to see him the minute he gets back, to be there when he arrives if I can find out when he's due.

Thursday, May 19, 2003 3:33 PM

I don't know if you remember me or not. I wrote to you last year after my son was killed in the crash of his Air Force plane. You wrote back to me several times. I wanted to take a moment to say thank you to your family for your son's service to our country. If you thought it would be a good idea, I would be grateful for his military address so that I could write him directly and say thank you.

They say that time heals all wounds. I am not so sure that is true. There is still a tremendous hole in my heart from the loss of my son. It doesn't hurt as much as it did but the sadness and the longing are still there. I visited his grave for the first time two weeks ago. It was very hard but what made it even harder was that day they were burying a soldier killed in the conflict and I saw the pain etched on the faces of his friends and family. . . .

On 8/7 my wife, stepdaughter, and son-in-law went to Ft. Logan for the first anniversary of Shane's death. Buried very close to him is a soldier by the name of Slocum who died in battle in Iraq. He was 23 years old. We placed flowers at his grave and prayed for him and his family. . . . One life well lived makes such a difference.

Dan Kimmett

Tuesday, May 24, 2003 10:03 PM

Have not heard from you in a while, has John gotten home yet? How are things with you on the home front these days? Billy got back to Norfolk and we met him at the base in style and gave his platoon a grand welcome home party. . . . Billy is being promoted to sergeant and will be helping to train the next Fast Company and have his own group of Marines.

Hope all is well, Frank,

Alan D. Ross

Thursday, May 26, 2003 12:00 PM

Subj: Wedding 30 August 2003

Hello, All,

After recently returning from Operation Iraqi Freedom, Peter and I came up with a date for our wedding. As you know, Peter and I got married last December but were unable to celebrate it with a reception. So, this is the official one! I know this is short notice and a lot of you are still deployed. However, Peter will be leaving again come December and we had to fit the date in this window of time. We will celebrate our wedding Saturday, 30 August, during the Labor Day weekend. I sincerely hope you can all attend. Details to follow, but save the day.

I hope to talk to you all soon!

Lt. Jane Vizzi Blair

May 29, 2003

Under the "Briefly Noted" heading in the *Times* today:

Afghanistan: Vehicle Attacked — Attackers set off a remote-controlled bomb near a vehicle carrying American Special Forces along Afghanistan's eastern border with Pakistan. . . . The bomb went off as the troops were on patrol . . . the spokesman said in a statement from Bagram Air Base.

The paper also reported that more troops would be deployed in Iraq for longer than anticipated. The countdown to John coming home is excruciating. I'm so superstitious that, when we were skiing, I never used to take "one more" run. I would quit while the going was good. When the kids said, "Just one more, Dad," I'd answer, "No. Quit while we're ahead." In this case words like "The last days of his deployment" seem to tempt fate.

Jessica and the children arrive tomorrow! I can't wait to see them but I know that the hazy layer of unease lying between the world and me will overshadow this visit. John may be coming home, but he's not home yet and the ache won't go away till he is. Today the copy-edited manuscript of *Zermatt* will arrive. I need to turn my novel around by the weekend. The summer project of fixing up the guest room will have to wait.

John called. He'll be back in three weeks if all goes well. He's lost about twenty pounds.

"No problem. I'm eating a lot now, five thousand calories a day."

"How many, uh, 'trips' have you been going on?"

"Oh, you know, now and again."

"Do you go in a chopper or in vehicles?"

"Both. But the driving is the interesting part. We drive civilian cars, SUVs, mostly commandeered from the Taliban, so they have bullet holes in them. Anyway, when you drive here it's, uh, 'interesting.' We don't stop or slow down for anything. If somebody tries to stop us we just go for it—we'll run them over if we have to. We go in convoys and have our procedure. But we never slow down because that's when they set off the roadside bombs. Anyway, when you drive here it's a whole different thing! Sometimes I'm the driver, sometimes the lookout. If someone appears threatening, we just point our guns at him till he stops being threatening." John laughed. "We say, 'If they run, then they're Al Qaeda. If they stand and face you, then they're *disciplined* Al Qaeda!' I got the box Mom sent, the candy and all. We'll take the toys to the children. . . ."

We had pictured John goofing off with his buddies with the kids' badminton sets and the horseshoe game Genie had sent. Now that I know it's all going to "John's kids," I wish we'd sent better toys. I've got to call Patrick and find out about John's car.

May 30, 2003

6:01 AM. Patrick called back and left a message: "I'll try and get this locked brake situation cleared up." Hooray for the Marine brotherhood! Jessica and the children arrive today. Genie is coming down with a cold. She is more stressed out than she admits.

In comparison to many other parents, Genie and I have it easy! John gets to call. He has not been wounded or killed. His job is dangerous but not as dangerous as some. He is writing poems and sending bits of prose that let us glimpse the state of his soul. There are a lot of military parents, wives, and husbands facing far, far worse.

41

Me, as if speaking of the holy of holies: "Benjamin, John's room is off-limits!"

My grandson, wide-eyed, breathless: "Yes, Grandpa, I won't touch anything of Uncle John's!"

Ben had come out of John's room clutching an ivory warthog tusk that John bought in the Johannesburg flea market. That's when I told Ben not to touch anything in John's room. I knew John wouldn't care. I can't help it.

John was eight, only a year older than Ben, when we lived in Africa for a year while I directed two movies. Ben was not perturbed by my instruction not to go into John's room. Moments later I heard Ben down in the living room cheerfully playing up a storm on the bongo drums he had brought with him from Finland.

Francis's and Jessica's rooms have long since been converted to other uses. But John's room is still filled with his childhood memorabilia.

Yesterday morning I showed Ben and Amanda the pictures from John's disposable cameras. My blond Scandinavian grandchildren leaned over me as I proudly showed them photographs of John with the cluster of Afghans their ages. They studied pictures taken out of several chopper doors. They asked about the other choppers in John's convoy, scrutinized blurred shots taken from moving vehicles, peered at bleak landscapes and ruined mud buildings, thin donkeys and emaciated camels and, of course, pictures of John, some in desert cammies, others in civilian clothes, posing with his buddies, armed, the bulky vest under his shirt making him look weirdly chunky, a sidearm strapped to his waist, an M-4 in his hands.

Amanda and Benjamin snuggled on my lap as I turned the pages. The sweet soap-and-water smell of their warm skin, the little arms around my neck, brought back a nostalgic longing. I suddenly ached for simpler times, when I was still the captain of the *Good Ship Schaeffer* and all my sailors were as safe as I could keep them. I shut my eyes and recalled how I'd swoop Jessica, Francis, and John up at the least excuse, their arms holding tightly around my neck as I carried them on my back, how we'd wrestle until we were completely disheveled and lay in a heap on the living room floor.

Afghanistan and Iraq were just footnotes in the children's encyclopedia back then, not the cause of my nightmares. War was something other people did. That was before my crew mutinied and, one by one, left for college, marriage, and war. The safe days, when the biggest challenges were doctor appointments, cut knees, soccer games, bills to pay, a living to earn, are fading into memory laced with guilt over too many angry words about so much that I now know was so trivial.

My grandchildren loved the pictures. I tried to imagine what it's like for them hearing the stories about their tall uncle, who they've not seen for four years, a child's lifetime. Jessica has a big photograph of John in his dress blues on their refrigerator. What a distant and legendary figure he must seem to children living in a peaceful old farmhouse in a little Finnish village!

I enjoy feeding the Corporal Schaeffer mythology, telling the next generation little bits of my conversations with him: about the bad guys John is helping to catch; about his leading the IC Pelicans to an undefeated basketball season; how beautiful his poems are; what he looked like tearing across the soccer field to stop an attacker. . . .

"See, Amanda, they would think they could score, had broken past the defense, but they never figured on how your uncle John could run! They didn't know he was a track star too! He could run down anybody, even if they were halfway to the goal and he was at midfield. He'd sprint and suddenly they'd see his shadow and turn!"

"But it was too late, wasn't it, Grandpa?"

"Yes, Amanda, those long legs were a blur! And next thing they knew he'd tapped the ball away and then cleared it the whole length of the field! And I could hear the other team's parents groan."

The kids remember the Twin Towers falling. Ben drew a picture of what he saw on TV, a plane crashing into a tower, flames and smoke. Jessica faxed it to me the day after the attack. On a second picture he'd drawn the towers again, still burning, but in his childish wobbly he hand also drew in ladders: "To help them all get out," he'd told Jessica.

The pictures were tucked behind a big chunk of pink quartz on the kitchen mantel, where we keep the thick wad of letters, drawings, cards, and other mementos too precious to toss. Ben's ladder had perfectly expressed my own anguish as I watched men and women fall and wished I could do something, anything, but sit paralyzed with horror.

I turned to the children as we looked at the last of the pictures John sent and said, "Your uncle is trying to stop those people from ever doing that to anyone again."

The children nodded. I didn't need to explain what "that" was.

42

Subj: 42 WET SHEEPDOGS
From: John Schaeffer

Hi to everyone! I've decided to start titling all my e-mails with completely nonsensical subjects, just so you don't expect to hear anything about 42 wet sheepdogs in this e-mail. If you do, you are about to be sorely disappointed, sorry.

I hope everybody's doing well. I am getting ready to come home and, barring unforeseen events, should begin that journey sometime circa the 15th of June (unless something comes up. I give it 50/50 odds), getting me there anywhere from the 17th to the 30th.

I'm a little busy right now, maybe you've seen something on the news and then again maybe you haven't, the American press being as ridiculously unreliable as it is. So I apologize for being out of touch; anyhow, all the best, and I'll catch up w/you all later.

J

June 5, 2003

I've been in New York for a few days with Amanda. Nothing is as comforting as walking up my beloved Upper West Side city sidewalks with the hand of my granddaughter thrust into mine. I took her to FAO Schwarz today and told her to pick out a favorite stuffed animal. Amanda narrowed her favorites down to three and was pondering which she liked "absolutely best," when I told her to take them all. Her eyes lit up. Heaven.

June 6, 2003

On the way home last night Amanda got carsick. Other than that, the trip was perfect. I cleaned up the car using my dirty laundry and the bottle of windshield fluid that was in the back. Twenty years ago something like this would have annoyed me. Not anymore! I don't even care that it's our new car and some of the vomit ran down inside the door panel; at the last moment she stuck her head out the window and missed! This is so easy! I'd pay a lot to have John back, age ten, getting sick in our car.

Genie, Jessica, Amanda, Benjamin, and I sat out in the screened porch and had dinner. Amanda regaled the family with our exploits. Best of all, she said, was the last stop on the way out of town at the Cloisters. I showed Amanda the wonderful gardens full of plants mentioned in medieval literature, the Unicorn Tapestries room, and the Campin *Annunciation Triptych*—the lovely three-panel devotional painting of Joseph building mousetraps in his workshop and Mary looking young and lovely, surrounded by the medieval symbols of virginity, including a white lily—and, of course, what I think of as "John's statue" of Mary and the baby Jesus.

At supper a skunk came waddling out of the bushes. I told everyone to sit still and raced upstairs for my shotgun. We'd had a skunk family get under the house a few years ago, and in the middle of the night one had "let off." We'd awoken, choking, sure the house was on fire. Skunk stink inside is a whole different experience than a whiff on the breeze!

When the skunk let off in the crawl space, some of the spray came up between the floorboards in the mudroom and, unknown to us, soaked John's school backpack. In the morning the house was stinking so strongly with throat-seizing stench that we didn't know what individual objects were more sprayed than others. John headed off with his sprayed backpack and got sickened by it after he arrived at school and was soon sent home by the school nurse.

I've been shooting the skunks that come into the garden ever since. The kids were not shocked as Grandpa blasted away. They're growing up in a Finnish village where farmers shoot moose, bear, and bobcats.

Amanda and Benjamin are asleep. The skunk is buried.

I read the paper. "Afghans Kill 40 Taliban Militants in Fierce Border Fights . . . increased rebel activity . . . daily fights between Taliban, Al Qaeda, and the American forces. . . . This week alone there were two major responses to Taliban resistance: in addition to the fighting Wednesday, American troops fought a major airborne assault operation on Monday. . . ." Maybe this was the action John was involved with that he said we'd soon read about in the press.

June 7, 2003

10:20 AM. We missed a call! John left a message.

"Hey, guys, it's me. If you see something on the news about an IED explosion in Kabul and about casualties and all that stuff, I'm fine. We went through there a few minutes later. We were lucky they didn't get us. Everything is all right with me, though some people have been killed. I'm fine. Love you."

Sunday, June 8, 2003

Afghanistan: Kabul Bombing
Kills 4 German Soldiers and Wounds 29

KABUL, Afghanistan (June 7) — A car packed with explosives pulled up to a bus carrying German peacekeepers in Kabul and detonated Saturday, killing four and wounding more than two dozen in the first fatal attack on the international force. . . .

7: 00 AM. The German soldiers were on their way to the airport for the flight home. They had just finished their tour of duty. It was a suicide attack by Al Qaeda. I never thought I'd tear up over German soldiers. My chest hurts. I want to go downstairs to see Jessica but feel when I write this diary I'm closer to John, illogically I suppose, as if the concentration of my thoughts can somehow protect him. They were killed on their way home.

Monday, June 9, 2003

Threats and Responses: Afghan Youth's
Death Raises Kabul Bombing Toll to Five

5:06 AM. Yesterday afternoon one of the little wire figures tumbled off my computer monitor. It was the writer with the quill. I put it back, of course, and the three little figures are sitting in a row again. I don't like that it fell off.

43

Now this group e-mail from John to all his friends . . .

Monday, June 9, 2003 4:29 AM
From: John Schaeffer
Subj: maybe/maybe not

Hey folks, things proceeding as expected. BUSY, however, I am taking a quick break just to prepare you all for the possibility that I may not be coming home as scheduled, thus this e-mail. Some things have come up recently which may force me to stay for a while longer than perhaps you had hoped.

Anyhow, it's not a definite either way but there is that possibility that I could be here up to 180 days as opposed to 90. Didn't want it to come on short notice, so I am throwing it out there as a hypothetical so everyone's in the loop. But I will let you know for sure when I find out.

Take care and I will see you all at some point in the next 3 weeks to 3 months. The only definite thing I can tell you is that I will certainly be back stateside by the end of September.

On the plus side the work is important. On the down side I am starting to get a little burnt out with no days off since March.

All the best,

J

Monday, June 9, 2003 5:54 AM
Subj: proud of you
From: Frank Schaeffer
To: John Schaeffer

John: I love you so very much and am so proud of what you are doing. Of course I'd rather have you home sooner than later. And I'm sad to think you may not be home when we thought. Hang in there! I miss you horribly. You are a much-loved guy, and not just by me but by all sorts of people.

Keep safe. Be careful and come home as quick as you can. Meanwhile keep us posted. If you are staying out there longer we'll send more treats! Let us know.

Love, *much* love,
Dad

I'll go downstairs to tell Genie now. I hear her grinding fresh coffee. The little wire man tumbling off the monitor was a bad omen after all. I'm so disappointed. In a minute I'll get up the courage to tell Genie.

7:26 AM. Genie had printed up the e-mail. John sent her a copy, of course. Before I plucked up the courage to tell her, she was already writing her reply. She looked so sad. John must be exhausted to the breaking point to even bring up the fact he's "a little burnt out." He never says he's tired, ever.

I had called Patrick to make sure the back wheels on John's car are working. I thought we'd need to have it ready in ten days. Now Patrick will almost be out of the service when John comes home. Who will watch over John's car? I'm obsessing about a ten-year-old car! My brain is turning to cottage cheese!

A few moments ago, while Amanda was taking a shower upstairs, the downstairs toilet overflowed and water and shit poured out on the

197

floor. The water from the shower had no place to go. The tank in the yard was full.

The grandchildren were amazed and horrified that something like this could happen. The switch on the pump that sends our sewage from the house up to the sewer line must have broken. I was able to pump the tank out using the manual override. I'm waiting for the pump guys to fix the system; all this because our house sits below the road where the city sewer runs, so we need a tank and a grinder pump to move our sewage to the road level. Luxury, thy name is a gravity-fed sewer line!

Forty people are coming to Francis's thirtieth birthday party this weekend. The pump *must* be fixed by then! I need to go out and buy the bottle of expensive Scotch John wants to get Francis; rather, instructed me to buy. I'm not a Scotch drinker. What's the right kind? Once you flush you're not supposed to see the harbinger of your decay again.

There were more names in the Sunday *Times,* names of the dead Americans killed last week in the "theater of operations": one here, two there, bad news in dribs and drabs, bad news backing up once we've "flushed." I have this terrible feeling that in the years ahead many more men and women will be killed "mopping up" than in the "official" war, two here, three there, rarely enough to make page one, just enough to shatter one heart at a time.

I don't want John's little figurines to tumble again! I want what I flush to stay flushed! I don't like reminders that my body is a biological time bomb literally full of crap. I hate mortality.

My Marine is way ahead of me. At boot camp all the doors were missing off the toilet stalls. There was no privacy, no pretense. Shit was shit! Shaved heads, going to the toilet in front of strangers, standing naked before the organized fury of the drill instructors, sent the message: You're nothing special, just one more recruit, and the mission comes first!

Now John is in Afghanistan with children that he's given the little joke toys to that we sent. Many of those kids won't see thirty. Life spans there are what they were in the tenth century in Europe. And here we think we'll live forever, but John has seen the shit and knows what we're made of. He saw the flag-draped coffins. And he was on base when Donald Rumsfeld went to Afghanistan and declared "major hostilities have ceased." But the killing is going on, in twos and threes, and in fours. The day before yesterday—when the Germans were on the way to the airport, fifteen minutes from getting the hell out, the day of joy for their fathers and mothers and wives and children turned into horror. The raw sewage poured out, stained hearts forever. If John had driven past a few moments earlier my world would have ended.

There is no tidy flushing. John left a message to say he was not coming home as planned, and meanwhile my pump was off and I didn't know it yet, and sewage was about to pour into our house. The war in Iraq is "over," Bush told us. Major operations in Afghanistan are "done," Rumsfeld said. Bush flew out to the aircraft carrier to tell us we'd won. We flush but it just comes back. And this morning, at this very moment at 0500, the DIs on Parris Island are rousting new recruits into wakefulness. They will shit in the open in front of each other. And some of them will lay down their lives for people whose idea of hardship is taking a trip without their personal masseuse. And if the war our Marines, soldiers, airmen, coastguard, and sailors die in is "over" or if the "sexy," newsworthy sound-bite action is some-place else, then they will only get their name listed on page sixteen in a little box about the size of the "Men Seeking Women" personals. And all the photo opportunities for the President and Secretary of Defense won't change the fact that the pipe is backing up.

I want John home before he makes that list! I want to pretend that when you flush, it just goes away! I want to pretend that John will live forever and that when you fix a pump it stays fixed! But I have this horrible feeling that all our military power won't save a lot of fathers and mothers from crying over sons' and daughters' graves.

44

8:30 AM. Jessica and the children are eating breakfast. John won't be home to see Jessica. Hillary Clinton just launched a massive publicity tour for her book; some say she wants to be president. Larry Craig, Republican senator from Idaho, is blocking Air Force promotions until the Idaho National Guard gets four more planes from the Air Force. That means people just like John serving in Iraq and Afghanistan are waiting for a small pay raise while this millionaire scumbag uses them as bargaining chips for his pork. There would have been more deaths in the attack on the German peacekeepers except for the fact that they were wearing their flak jackets. John, wear your vest! An Afghan boy also died in the hospital today from the attack. "John's children" are also paying a price. If Chelsea Clinton was out in the desert with John, maybe I'd want to read Hillary's book.

10:51 AM. I heard a garbled message. I think John was trying to get through. I was outside helping the guy pull the grinder pump out of the tank. We're going to have to replace the system. This is one bad day! Genie is driving the grandchildren and Jessica down to see Francis. They'll spend the afternoon where toilets flush. I'll hang around inside to see if John calls back.

I remember joking with John before he left.

Me: "John, I might follow you over there. Maybe you'll see me waving from a hilltop."

John: "If you do, I'll fuckin' shoot you!"

Right now I'm almost willing to risk it!

Reading between the lines of John's e-mail, he's not only exhausted, he's discouraged, a little melancholy. I love you, son. I'd pay a thousand bucks to be able to cook you dinner tonight.

Happy thought: maybe the extra time "over there" will help John resolve to get the hell out of the military when the time rolls around to re-up. I admire my hero. I love the United States Marines. I'm prouder of my Marine's service than of anything *I've* ever done. And I *never want to go through this again!*

Tuesday, June 10, 2003 1:24 PM
Subj: Returned to America from Iraq
    Hello, everyone,
    I just wanted to let you know that I arrived safely back in America. Peter and I are still planning on having a wedding celebration and we are looking at dates. Thanks for all the support while I was deployed. I look forward to talking to you all soon. Expect a wedding invitation in the mail!
    All the best,
    Jane Vizzi Blair

Saturday, June 7, 2003 6:44 AM
    We have info that our son, Cpl. Daniel Beach, will be flying

into California sometime Sunday! Of course, we are still here in beautiful Beaufort, SC. But we are rejoicing that he will be stateside. His wife of one year is here with her parents. . . . His general told them all no leave until maybe August. We will have our hero's welcome then. I never mentioned that he married his sweetheart last June 29th. They have known each other all their teen life. . . .

Here in Beaufort, many Marines (and sailors) have returned to their families. I rejoice with them. Only one was lost. A retired Marine has set up a fund to help support his yet unborn daughter. A sad story of two (wife, also) left behind but a good story of one Marine looking out for the other. Many have donated to the cause.

As one Marine father to another, I'm wishing you a reunion soon with your son.

Chuck Beach

Saturday, June 9, 2003 5:08 AM

Dear Chuck:

I'm so glad your son will be home soon. It looks like John's deployment got extended till September. So we're a little sad because we thought he would be on the way home by the end of June. Some people don't realize that whole families go into the military even if only one of them is wearing the uniform!

Best,

Frank

In *Leatherneck* there was an article about some new medals that will be given to American military personnel who are fighting in the war on terror. There are four new medals. John will get some to add to his other service ribbons. If—*when!*—he gets back, I want to see him in his dress blues with those ribbons!

5:33 AM. Jessica helped me yesterday, like old times. She works so well. She is a magnificent mother and woman, yet is still my little girl, looking a bit nervous while we nailed up plywood. Was she trying to do it right for Daddy in case he yelled? I cringe looking back at how impatient I was with my kids, especially with Jessica, the first to test the waters of my then nonexistent parental skills.

While Jessica and I worked, Amanda and Benjamin were down by the river at the small sandy strip of beach they love. I gave them an old fish trap. They baited it with bread and stuck it in one of the pools that dot the marsh grass. In a few hours it was full of little fish and one eel. The kids kept them alive all day by changing the water in the plastic tank they put them in, and at the end of a long, hot, sunny day, they returned the fish no worse for wear to the marsh pool.

Late in the afternoon I got an old rod out of the barn and took the kids down to the river to fish. We didn't catch anything. It was the first time I'd fished from the bank since John was a kid. In all the years we fished off our riverbank, and once in a while out of our little rowboat, we only kept and ate three or four stripers out of the dozens we caught. John always let them go.

One night during his last summer before boot camp, several years after we quit fishing together, John was awake and wandering around, going for one of his long, solitary, restless rambles, when he spotted some huge stripers feeding under the bridge. He scavenged around trying to find the old rods, but they were upstairs in the barn. In the morning I saw some string with a safety pin tied to it lying on our big old kitchen table. I asked John what it was for. He said that he'd gotten the urge to try and catch one of those fish, that they had been in some sort of a feeding frenzy, and he "had to try." He didn't get one, though. Maybe it was because the only bait he could find was some bacon.

Another U.S. soldier has been killed in Iraq, another name on the growing list since the war "ended." I've put the rod and net in the garden toolshed, where it is easy to find. When John comes home, I'll tell him where it is in case he wants to fish.

6:02 AM. Another group e-mail from John . . .

From: John Schaeffer
Wednesday, June 11, 2003 4:35 AM
Subj: staying a while
Well, ladies and gents, I will in fact be staying in country a while longer than had been anticipated. For various reasons I will remain here until things are well enough in hand to pass on to my replacement. Hopefully this will be before September or I will have to hand them off, ready or not, as I will have to return to the States. This due to the policy of the intel outfit.
If this makes any of you nervous, then I can only say this: "Rumors of my demise are greatly exaggerated." And if any of you are hoping that these rumors are not greatly exaggerated, then you can kiss my ass! Don't know exactly when things will be set, but will keep you all posted as I can.
John

Wednesday, June 11, 2003 6:16 AM
From: Frank Schaeffer
To: John Schaeffer
Subj: Re: staying a while
Hey, son: Give us a call sometime. We are all sorry as hell you're not on the way home but proud that you are the indispensable man! I talked to Patrick and your car is fixed so it'll be ready when you are. Patrick will make sure to leave the

emergency brake off this time, so the back wheels won't freeze up again! Meanwhile, we still can't flush the toilets. The new pump is supposed to be in today! Great timing, huh? With Jessica and the kids here we sort of need the toilets!

I love you,

Dad

U.S. TROOPS IN AFGHANISTAN KILL
4 TALIBAN SUSPECTS NEAR BORDER

KABUL, Afghanistan, June 10 — American troops killed four suspected Taliban members in a three-hour gun battle on the Pakistani border, a military spokesman said today. The soldiers were on patrol when they came under attack shortly before dawn today, Col. Rodney Davis said. There were no American casualties. . . .

June 12, 2003

5:54 AM. I put out the garbage; rather, dragged the two cans up the drive. One was heavy, filled with the sodden, stinking towels from the overflow cleanup. The men will come to install the new pump this morning, *I hope!* I've been pissing in the bushes. Genie, Jessica, and the kids visit friends with working toilets.

The *Times* lay like a little blue landmine in its innocuous wrapper. Will John try and call on Francis's birthday on Saturday? What headlines will explode in my face?

I love having the grandchildren here, but I'm distracted. It's more like hearing about their visit than actually experiencing it. When Francis was at Georgetown, I missed him terribly but months felt like months, not lifetimes. With Jessica living in Finland, I long to see her and her children, but a year between visits seems shorter than a week of John's deployment.

John stands in black-and-white. He's wearing his sleeveless "muscle" undershirt. He looks like an uncomplicated young star out of some 1940s movie, or a handsome field worker in a tent city in *The Grapes of Wrath*. He had just come home from his base in Arizona for a visit when the picture was snapped. We stood on our deck side by side as he draped his muscular arm over my shoulder. John was looking down at me with wry amusement and smiling tenderly. There was love in that look. How long can a father hold his son in memory? John is becoming such a distant figure as the weeks drag into months. My shoulders ache for that arm to be draped over them. A casual gesture snapped in a second now seems like a luxury.

As I pass the picture while I climb the stairs to our bedroom, I always touch it. And I always glance at the picture of my grandfather Schaeffer in his Navy uniform, taken in 1898, that sits next to the photograph of John and me. I've put the photographs side by side. I never met my dad's father. I have no feelings for him except a vague interest in trying to understand the similarity between his face and his great grandson's. John looks like Grandfather.

When John enlisted I gave him Grandfather Schaeffer's June 14, 1898, honorable discharge certificate from the U.S. Navy. "You earned this," I said. "I never served. It should be yours." Before John left for boot camp he turned it to the wall so the light wouldn't further fade the old document.

John missed his great grandfather by more than seventy years. My granddaughter is ten and I'm fifty. Maybe I'll meet some great grandchildren and they'll remember me. Did my grandfather know he'd be so thoroughly forgotten, reduced to one photo and a document on which the ink is fading?

"There is no remembrance of former things, nor will there be any remembrance of things that are to come by those who will come after. . . ." (Ecclesiastes 1:11)

June 14, 2003

5:14 AM. I show Genie the cover photo of today's *Times*. It's of a kneeling American soldier comforting another kneeling soldier bowed with grief. The caption reads: BRIAN PACHOLSKI, A MILITARY POLICE OFFICER, COMFORTED A FRIEND, DAVID BORELLO, WHO BROKE DOWN YESTERDAY AFTER SEEING THREE IRAQI CHILDREN INJURED WHILE PLAYING WITH EXPLOSIVES NEAR BAGHDAD. . . .

Genie is downstairs making porcini tarts for the party. Sitting in the kitchen is the little pile of presents from John for Francis: the chess set he sent from Afghanistan, the two bottles of Scotch I bought yesterday, and the joke present for his "over-the-hill" brother—Depends adult diapers.

Saturday, June 14, 2003 10:31 AM
September? I'm so sorry! Poor John! We're praying for his safe return. Ski will probably want to hold off taking leave until Shaf returns, he only wanted to take leave to spend time with him. Ski never takes leave; he didn't even take leave for our anniversary. Luckily, it fell on his day off! I'll have to check if Sgt. Emily Johnson has more pictures of your son and Ski together in Ft. Huachuca (Ft. We Gotcha!)
Mrs. "Ski" (Rachael Ludwikowski)

7:59 PM. Genie and I come back from a walk over to town.

Jessica says John called. She reports that he sounded tired but fine. He told her that he could have left but that the two new guys in charge of his operation just arrived and have no idea what is going on yet. He said, "Bad things happen when mistakes are made," so, as John explained, he'd stay and help train them. It would have been "irresponsible to leave now," John told Jessica. He said the new officers were glad he volunteered to stay. "Once they're settled in I can come home."

John talked to the grandchildren and dictated some funny things to put on Francis's birthday card. He said he'd try to call during the party.

June 16, 2003

6:05 AM. Yesterday I spent most of the party in the kitchen serving food, hiding from Francis's friends, mostly his students, fellow teachers, and their parents from the Waring School. They are all terrifically good company. Usually I would have loved to be with them. Francis saw I was depressed and did everything he could to cheer me up. From time to time, the parents and students popped into the kitchen to tell me about all the inspiration Francis brings into their lives. I'm so proud of Francis, but my mind kept veering into gloomy territory. It was a buffet-style spread and I pretended I needed to be inside serving, even when everyone was served. I was waiting for John's call, if any. I knew John would say I was being silly. But any missed call looms large to me.

After the party I put the chaise-longue deck chair we gave Francis in our truck and drove to his apartment on the Waring School campus. Francis and I wrestled it from my truck up the back exterior fire escape to his second-floor deck.

"That was a great party, Dad, thanks," Francis said cheerfully, as we carried the chair.

"No, it wasn't. I sulked in the kitchen. I'm sorry."

"That's okay. I know you're worried."

"Yes, but well, it's not logical to blow off your party. What's the point of worrying for one son when the other son you love is right there to enjoy?"

"I still had a great time."

At around four the call finally came and I raced out to get Francis, let them talk, then after about five minutes picked up to say hello. John was giving Francis a rundown of events.

". . . We have a thirteen-year-old at the school teaching the kids because he speaks English. . . . The girls are unbelievably happy because they get to go to school. . . . Also we fund an orphanage. In Muslim countries, at least here in Afghanistan, they can't adopt or something, so if you're a kid in an orphanage you're stuck. . . . Adults can take kids in but they can never be their child, get their name. . . . So people don't take the kids, so they are stuck in the orphanage. . . . Children sometimes get adopted in a sense, but never into the family, never in the legal sense. . . . Finished work at about seven AM, slept till noon, till it was about one hundred and twenty in the tent and one hundred outside. . . . An IED went off again. . . . They use these remote mines a lot, set them off with cell phones when our guys drive by. . . . But they have to be close by to do it, so they can see when our vehicles pull even with the IED. . . . So if they miss us we get them. . . . How? [laughter] Some guy is standing in the middle of an otherwise empty road with a phone in his hand and a bomb just went off, so we kinda know what happened! I love you guys. . . . Happy birthday, Francis. . . ."

45

5:24 AM. I'm going to drive Ben to New York City. He has his bongo drums ready and a sign he laboriously hand-lettered on cardboard in the best tradition of panhandling: STARTED PLAYING POTS AND PANS WHEN I WAS 1, NOW I NEED MONEY FOR GROWN-UP DRUMS. In his accented little high-pitched voice he announced he wants to play on the street and/or in the subway and "make a little money." He came up with the sign all by himself. My grandson, the seven-year-old street musician! We're both excited.

The fog of depression lifted when I called Frank and told him that I was having a tough time enjoying my grandchildren. The good sense of Frank's response hit home: "Enjoy your daughter and grandchildren's visit. You don't help John by worrying about him. But of course you know all that. Cut it out!"

I had been talking about taking Ben to New York but was too depressed. After talking to Frank I announced, "We're going tomorrow!" Ben smiled an immense smile. Will I get arrested on some child labor charge? John would like this adventure.

Ten more Americans were injured in Iraq, three seriously. Genie and the children went shopping for more candy, toys, and school supplies to send to John for the Afghan children. Before supper last night I was telling Genie about the fact that ten more

Americans had been injured. Benjamin chimed in with his chirpy little voice: "Was it John?"

"No," I said, "he's fine."

June 18, 2003

11:20 PM. New York City: Correcting the typeset proofs of *Zermatt*, the radio set to 96.3 FM. Ben is asleep.

At 11:05 PM they played my favorite piece by Suk: *Serenade for Strings*. My grandson sleeps next to me, covers kicked off. Suk wrote *Serenade* to mourn the death of his beloved young wife. The poignant melody envelops me. I receive *Serenade* as a promise that beauty still trumps despair.

June 20, 2003

Thursday, June 19, 2003 7:22 AM
From: John Schaeffer
Subj: home?

Hey, dad, don't have much time, kinda busy. Anyhow, looks like I might be able to get back in time to catch Jessa after all for the tail end of her visit. Small chance, so don't tell anyone, not Mom, nobody. Sorry, in a rush.

Love, John

Thursday, June 19, 2003 8:25 AM
From: Frank Schaeffer
Subj: Re: home?

John: I love you lots! I won't tell but I'll sure be praying you do get home soon. Let me know what you need.

Love you,
Dad

I'm still in NYC with Ben. It's my wedding anniversary. After I realized I'd just said I'd take Ben to the city and be away from home on the day, Genie read my mind and said, "We can celebrate later."

Last night Ben and I had a splendid time! Ben played his bongos in Times Square and in front of Lincoln Center. He earned twenty-six dollars in about ten minutes! I kept chickening out and moving locations. Maybe this child labor deal is something I should look into after all! At this rate we could clear a thousand dollars a day!

Ben is small for seven. He is a wonder on those bongos and, because he looks a year younger than he is, the combination of his size, cute face, mop of wispy blond hair, and precocious talent is irresistible. Ben has certainly inherited his brilliant jazz musician–composer father's gift. Seen-everything New Yorkers stopped dead in their tracks to watch, and a steady stream of dollars dropped on Ben's denim jacket. He was too shy to look up to meet anyone's gaze and just kept drumming for dear life. I hung around the edges and snapped pictures. People did a double take when they heard the elegant complex rhythms. I think they expected to see some old professional. Their eyes snapped open wide when they spotted Ben crouched over those drums. Later, on the phone to Jessica, I heard Ben chirp, "No, Mom, the cops were no problem! Only the security guards at Lincoln Center gave us any trouble!"

We met my editor, Will, and hung around the Upper West Side with his lovely wife, Karen, and their two charming daughters, seven and three. The Balliett daughters were shy through dinner, but later, when they heard Ben play, the three children began to troop around together like old friends.

There was a master class for jazz guitarists, about a dozen men playing with their teacher, jazz guitarist Bob Brosman, in the quad of Columbia University. When they spotted Ben with his bongos, they invited him to accompany them. He did. He provided the rhythm to a complicated jazz/salsa tune with all the guitarists sitting around him playing and staring at him.

As Will commented later over ice cream, it was like some scene from a Hollywood movie, where a kid sneaks into Madison Square Garden and is allowed to shoot a few hoops with the team and ends up dunking on Shaq in that night's game. My son may be coming home sooner than I thought! My grandson has his father's talent and is a sweet, polite boy too! Life is good! Victory to my Marines and confusion to their enemies!

This magical moment in the greatest city on earth is what John is fighting for. This is the New York that was attacked, the city where a kid from the other side of the world can wander into the quad at Columbia, less than ten blocks from the Duke Ellington Memorial, and hear, see, and join in with some of the world's greatest jazz guitarists, then skip away feeling as if he's walking on air. This is freedom.

June 22, 2003

7:24 AM. Genie has taken Jessica, my son-in-law, Dani, and the grandchildren to the Cape for the Walsh family reunion. I'm staying home till Tuesday, when I'll join them. It's Sunday. I need a few days to catch up on some work, but mainly to clear my head. I'm frazzled!

Yesterday Genie wanted to take the recent family pictures, about a year's worth, to show her family. They were not in albums yet. While Genie had lunch with Jessica and the grandchildren I disappeared into our bedroom and slipped hundreds of photographs into the cellophane pockets filling two albums.

I hurried. The albums went to the Walsh reunion as mixed-up as our lives: a jumble of birthdays, visits to New York, war, Afghanistan, bongos in Times Square, more war in Afghanistan, Francis's birthday party, John in his dress blues on *Nightline,* John's pile of equipment in his barracks just before he shipped out, the close-ups of the vest and atropine injectors, Francis coaching his soccer team, Jessica with the children on a rocky island in Finland, the last pictures of John stateside in his polar bear pajamas. . . .

4:14 PM. And all of a sudden a roundabout message from John! The P.S. to me is so typically and maddeningly laid-back for big news. . . .

Sunday, June 22, 2003 10:24 AM
Subj: Frank Schaeffer
From: John Schaeffer
   Dear Mr. O'Connor,
   My father forwarded me the note you wrote him [about *Keeping Faith* and Mr. O'Connor's son becoming a Marine] and I am writing to congratulate both your son for his outstanding motivation and performance throughout his Marine Corps life thus far and also to congratulate your wife and yourself. The Marine Corps can change a great deal in a person but it must build upon bedrock that is already there. To continue on through the first 28 days of training *twice* is no small feat (the first month is widely considered the worst of boot camp, and I doubt that I could have done it), especially after an extended stay in medical recovery hell, and it speaks extremely well of both your son as a man, and you as a parent.
   I understand that the order of training has been moved around a little since I was on Parris Island in '99. However, judging from the quality of the junior Marines it has been my everlasting privilege to lead at home and abroad, the substance of the training has in no way been diminished.
   I will be returning from a deployment soon and am looking forward to seeing my family, especially my older sister and her children, whom I have not seen for four years. I'm very glad that our book was helpful to you. You are the people for which it was meant and I'm glad you say it provided an insight into

the kinship that your son and I, although we will probably never meet, will share forever, even as far as guarding the gates of Heaven, if the hymn is correct. (Ask your son what it means if that line mystifies you.) I wish you and yours the very best in what must be a time of great pride and joy for you.

Very Respectfully,

John Schaeffer (CPL/USMC)

Semper Fi

P.S. You may notice in the courtesy copy line that I have included two separate addresses; please do not think that I am sending this e-mail to someone you would not be comfortable having read your mail. Both addresses are my father's. I CC him on things like this so that my family will know that I am fine, as I'm a little bit pressed for time and will not be able to contact him any other way today. So I'm also going to tack something on for my parents real quick.

Dad, I'll be home on the Fourth of July, almost definitely, will contact you with details, ran out of time to write, sorry, love to everyone.

46

Sunday, June 22, 2003 4:43 PM
From: Frank Schaeffer
To: John Schaeffer
Subj: See you on the second!

Hey, Big Guy! I'm booking a flight down to BWI on the second of July. That way I'll be there on the third to drive home with you. A) I'll get to see you. B) You can get some sleep and not crash the car. If for any reason your plans change, it doesn't matter because I'll just use the ticket some other time and it'll still be good.

What I'll do is check into a motel so you can get your stuff together. Then I'll call Patrick and the duty desk and tell them where I am. When you want to contact me they'll know how. If you have any updated information, let me know.

Love,
Dad

5:06 PM. I've booked a one-way ticket to Baltimore. I'll fly down on the second, meet John, then drive back with him. I don't want him to get this far, then fall asleep at the wheel. The German peacekeepers were blown up on the way to the airport. Please, Lord, please.

11.38 PM. It's hard to get to sleep. With John coming home, I keep thinking about how we should greet him. Will he want things quiet? Will he want a party? How do we welcome our returning warrior?

Genie says wait. Give John a few days, then have a party for him. I agree. Another soldier died in Iraq today. Jane called. She and her husband Peter will have their wedding reception—at last!—on August 30 in Miami. My Marines are coming home! I feel shy about seeing John.

Monday, June 23, 2003 7:33 AM
From: John Schaeffer
Subj: Re: See you on the second!

Hey, dad, do me a favor and have Mom reactivate my cell phone on the first, that way it will be up and running when I get back. Also please ask Pat to get the oil changed in the car (as it is later in the pay period he is probably running short on the funds, so please offer to send him the money, from my account, should he need it) and ask him to drive it around quite extensively to loosen it up a little, as I want it running smoothly on the way up the coast. Also tell him that I will shoot him an e-mail at his work address with times I am coming back, and ask him to organize for someone to get me if he can't do it himself.

I don't want you to come down to meet me, not because I don't want to see you but because A: I am coming from the other side of the planet on a straight shot and will be pissed, jet-lagged, and just tired of dealing with anything that doesn't have to do with a shower and a bed. B: I will be working straight on the 3rd to get ready to leave and sleeping that afternoon in preparation for the night drive, which actually makes more sense for me because I will still be operating on Afghan time and missing holiday traffic. Thus I would not see you until about

0100 or so on the Fourth, when I would be picking you up and heading north, effectively defeating any reason to fly south and sit around for two days to get in a car at 1 am and drive. I will see you soon enough and you don't want to be around me when I get off this plane! I will be tense without my weapon and will probably be spun up all to hell wondering where I am.

So just hold your horses and I will come to meet you. Will you still be on the Cape at the Walsh reunion? I can drive straight there if you would like, just give me directions from the Mass Pike and I'll show up in the morning on the Fourth.

Love,

J

Monday, June 23, 2003 8:08 AM
From: Frank Schaeffer
Subj: Re: See you on the second!

John! How great you're on your way! I won't fly down. I get it. No problem. I have a call in to Patrick already re the car. Last I heard he got the wheels unlocked. We will all be home from the Cape by the 4th, so come straight home. I'll get Genie onto the phone issue today. Let me know what else we can do. Also I'll confirm with Patrick that your car is working.

Love, Dad

June 23, 2003

8:43 AM. I'm on hold with Sprint, reactivating John's cell phone. I'm pushing all the wrong buttons. I'm shunted from one computer voice to another. I'm worrying that he'll fall asleep at the wheel. Everything seems loud and magnified by his arrival. I hate Sprint!

Monday, June 23, 2003 12:54 PM

Frank: John coming home is good news. And thank you for your kind words.

[In answer to your question] "okay" is the right word to use. Although there will always be a sense of tremendous loss, we have been able to focus on the good that not only Shane did but the good that other people do every day. I never realized I had so many friends until Shane was killed. My healing has been greatly affected by them. I think of John often and pray that he will be safe. I will write him and tell him how much I appreciate his sacrifice and duty.

I am so glad that you will have him home very soon. I forgot to mention that the Social Security Administration stopped sending my daughter-in-law the benefits that she was entitled to. She did get it straightened out but it took some time. The Florida state government has given her free tuition to attend graduate school at the University of Florida. Most of her friends' husbands have been on duty in Iraq. Thankfully, it appears that they will all come home safely.

I was able to visit Shane's grave. . . . I stayed with him for over an hour and told him how proud we all were and how much we love him. In one sense it was very hard to go to the grave. I have a hard time thinking of him lying there. In another sense it was very good for me. I truly believe that he is in a better place and that we all will be together again someday.

My mother and father never recovered from his loss. Shane was their first grandchild and had a very special place in their hearts. My dad is a veteran and they have reserved sites near Shane's so that they can rest with him when the time comes. . . .

His cousin Cpl. Allen Leiper serves with the 3rd Marine Expeditionary Force and was in country during the war.

Thankfully he is all right. He too took Shane's death very hard since they had grown up together.

Your thoughts and prayers are very welcome by our family. It is so good to know that our friends think of him often and hold him in their hearts.

Dan Kimmett

June 28, 2003

I just got home from the Walsh family reunion. It was lovely, though we all missed Genie's Mom and Dad, since Stan had to stay in California while he undergoes radiation therapy. Then this: a copy of an e-mail letter to John that Dan sent.

Monday, June 23, 2003 4:01 PM
To: Cpl. John Schaeffer, USMC
Subject: Thank you
John,

You do not know me. I am one of those people in the States that you protect every day. I just wanted you to know how much I appreciate your service to our country and more specifically to my family and I.

My son, SSGT Shane Kimmett, was killed on August 6, 2002, when his Combat Talon II aircraft hit a mountain during flight. They were flying in very poor weather and his plane flew at 200' off of the deck and at 300 knots. While trying to insert Special Forces soldiers into an LZ they hit the side of the mountain.

Shortly after my son's death I read an article written by your dad and it meant something very special to me. I wrote him and he was kind to reply. He told me about your service and I have often kept you in my thoughts and prayers. . . .

Please know just how much we all appreciate your devotion
to duty and the sacrifice that you make daily on our behalf.
Yours gratefully,
Dan Kimmett

June 29, 2003

2:42 PM. John called from Uzbekistan! He is out of Afghanistan! He
is on his way home! I took the call in the living room and my two
grandchildren were there listening, eyes wide. I motioned them to
race upstairs and wake Genie, napping after our Sunday lunch. We
both got on the phone.

"I just had the best meal I've had in three years. I had thinly
sliced onions with crisp beef. I started with a great glass of white
wine. For dessert I had some fruit sorbet. There is green grass here! I
haven't seen green for four months!"

"Sounds great," said Genie.

John chuckled.

"The grass spooks me because I keep thinking that with grass I
can't see mines!"

"When do you come home?" I asked.

"I'll be here one night, then I fly to Germany and I'll call you
from there. Dad, I'm bringing you a whip the Taliban morality police
used to beat men with when they didn't grow beards, and a burka for
you, Mom!" John laughed.

"Did my last box get there?" asked Genie.

"The presents arrived that you sent for the schoolchildren. Was
that the last box?"

"Yes," said Genie.

"I got the box the last day and it will all be distributed. They love
pens—you give a kid a pen and then he's somebody. They'd rather
have pens than money. Anyway, I should be home on the Fourth of

July, if all goes well. I'm already nervous, no body armor or weapons!" John chuckled.

"I'll be there!" I said.

"Dad, don't drive down. I'll need the drive to just get used to being back."

"Hey, you'll be tired. I don't want you falling asleep at the wheel!" I said.

"Don't worry about the drive; I've just graduated from the most advanced driving school in the world—Afghanistan! I love you guys and will see you in, what? Four days? Love you. . . ."

47

Monday, June 30, 2003 12:20 AM
From: John Schaeffer
Subj: Uzbekistan
   Hey,
   Uzbekistan is pretty cool. I think I'll just stay here! Enjoying
the first day off I've had in 4 months and I'm doing it in a very
scenic country! Of course I planned on sleeping in but I woke
up exactly on time at 0400 this morning. Good times, good
times. Oh well.
   See ya,
   J

June 30, 2003

4:37 AM. Huge signs? Marine flags? Yellow ribbons everywhere?
None of this seems to be a good fit for my quiet hero. He has invited
over his friends via e-mail, we'll leave it at that and cook favorite
foods and put up a big American flag on the deck. My grandchildren
are waiting and Jessica, who has taken a little trip with Dani, will be
home by midday on the Fourth. Francis is going to drive up as soon
as we get word to him that John is home.

5:01 PM. Benjamin is watching *Groundhog Day,* a John favorite. Amanda is downstairs asleep. She has the flu. I'm sitting at my desk thinking about what it meant to walk in my front door, after running some errands, and see John's battered, dusty olive green seabag sitting like a promise of my son's imminent arrival. The postman had just dropped it off. According to the customs tags, the seabag came through JFK by post, marked "Priority." It smells musty. I last saw this seabag in John's barracks. It was new then. The label and customs declaration are in John's unmistakable spidery hand. I went into John's room, where I stowed it on his bed, checked the bag, again, studied the label, again, and then hugged the bag.

July 1, 2003

12:17 PM. Amanda is back from the doctor. John is in Germany, I hope! If the last plan holds, he'll be flying to the USA tomorrow. I've put the picture of my son holding an Afghan child, up on the wall of the staircase. John has been in harm's way, not only for our country's sake but for the Afghan people we've somewhat liberated— at least temporarily—from a political/religious cult of misogynistic oppression. Little girls are allowed to go to school now, at least in the small area of the country we actually control. I want each of the children in the picture to succeed; to live in a better world, to be freer and live longer lives. One in five Afghan children die before they are ten. John held a few of those children in his arms. They are related to me in some way now.

July 2, 2003

6:50 AM. I can't get used to not being afraid. Amanda is sleeping in the living room, sick with a sore throat and fever. It's a beautiful day, clear air, hot, sunny. My faith is shaky this morning. It just does not explain enough. There seem to be two meanings: the religious one I cling to, and the impersonal unknowable I sometimes suspect is closer to reality. It's easy to get bound up in each moment, as if all the personal striving is important. But when I look up, look around, I realize that all my little activities are just so much busywork and posturing. What is the real meaning? I'm not sure.

We humans give each other prizes at Oscar time, write glowing or damning book reviews, put each other in prison for breaking laws we make up, go to war, send our sons and daughters off to die, struggle to make ends meet, to get rich, to become powerful. And most people spend all their lives scratching out a meager existence. Maybe there is no "why."

Only love contradicts the void. Love is the one thing that motivates actions that can't be cynically explained away as mere survival instinct. I don't understand anything this morning, but I feel love in sharp stabs. John is coming home! Maybe that is enough meaning for a lifetime.

8:46 PM. John called from Detroit! Two hours later he called from Baltimore! Genie took both calls and reported. She was glowing and looking dazed. "He says he's so out of it, so tired. But he sounded fine. . . ."

John is back on U.S. soil! God bless America!

Wednesday, July 02, 2003 6:05 PM

To All: As of four PM today, July 2nd, John Schaeffer, Marine and beloved son, made it back to the USA after four months of deployment in the Middle East. We, his mom and dad, are greatly relieved, thankful to God and proud of our son. We are also mindful as never before of the other parents, husbands, and wives of those still in harm's way while they serve our country and watch our backs. We grieve for those who will not be coming home.

WELCOME HOME, SON! WELL DONE! Victory to our armed forces, confusion to their enemies!

All the very best,

Genie and Frank Schaeffer

Wednesday, July 02, 2003 11:16 PM

Congratulations on your son's homecoming. I'm smiling now, thinking how joyous an occasion this is for you. Thank God he returned safely. We are anticipating Mike's return on July 4 around 1:30 pm. We will rest much easier when he is actually here and we'll have fireworks to celebrate!

Sincerely,

Karen Hill

From: Frank Gruber

To: Frank Schaeffer

Wednesday, July 2, 2003 1:28 PM

Wonderful! I'll call you tomorrow.

Much love,

Frank

48

July 3, 2003

5:17 AM. My brain is still in fight-or-flight mode. I don't think I have any blood left in my veins. I seem to pump nothing but adrenaline. I'm so excited, but the almost unbearable surge of emotion feels like panic. Maybe when I see the boy I'll feel better.

Yesterday a Marine was killed in Baghdad. A soldier died in the hospital from his wounds. A Shia cleric issued a *fatwa* against the Americans. A grenade was thrown at the Marine. Where is Asher Boucher?

> *Thursday, July 3, 2003 12:48 AM*
> WELCOME BACK, SHAF! I MISSED YOU, BROTHER!
> LCpl "Ski" Ludwikowski

> *Thursday, July 3, 2003 7:06 AM*
> I rejoice with you on your son's return. I am still rejoicing on my son's return, as well (even though I have not seen him yet). We are two blessed dads. Unfortunately, many parents cannot celebrate this homecoming of our heroes. . . . I think July 4th now has an enlightened meaning to me. . . .

Have a wonderful reunion with your son.

Chuck Beach

P.S. If John is ever stationed here in Beautiful Beaufort, I'll be more than glad to provide as much hospitality as I can for him.

Thursday, July 3, 2003 9:19 AM

I am so happy for your family! Surely one of the highest times in your life! I look forward to our son's return. We found out a week ago that he would be leaving Karbala for Baghdad. How clearly I remember that day last summer when Austin called me at work and said, "Mom, I'm going to join the Marines."

Sincerely,

Jeannine Hubbell

49

July 4, 2003

4:31 AM. "I'm on my cell. It's working!" John said, and laughed. "I'm about half an hour out, just passing the Lawrence exit. . . . Check the lawn for mines, Dad! Better yet, pave the garden over! And while you're at it, buy me some body armor and a sidearm! I feel naked!"

<hr>

5:00 AM. A tall, thin figure slowly unfolds from our old car. I give Genie a head start. Mother embraces son.

"I was so worried," said Genie.

John holds her and she sobs.

Her face presses on his olive green T-shirt and leaves an imprinted tearstain as she pulls away to look up. Then it's my turn. He smells like cigarettes and is warm from the car, stretching now from sitting for eight hours. Hard arms hug me. The sharp stones on the driveway cut into my bare feet, reassuring me that I'm awake and actually holding on to my son.

<hr>

I sat with John while he undressed for his shower. He was wearing a little cross with his dog tags. "I'm a Catholic, please call a priest" is inscribed on the back. John said he found it at Bagram Air Base and showed it to us while we were still out on the driveway, clearly one of his most important possessions.

"Since there are no Orthodox priests or chaplains out there, it was the next best thing," he said with a grin.

9:29 PM. It was a perfect Fourth of July. In the morning John and I sat on his bed as he talked about hours worked and missions about which I'll never know more than that they were "very interesting, a little too interesting, sometimes." John talked about how the Afghans are never going to make a nation out of their "many warring tribes. . . ."

I only thought about it later but realized that Genie gave me a great gift by allowing me time alone with John. He was bone weary and kept stretching out—then sitting up again to say something. I sat next to him and made sure I was gripping him the whole time, an arm, foot, hand; it didn't matter, I just wanted to be certain that the nightmares were lies.

John's eyelids were drooping. He'd speak, fall silent, doze off, rouse himself, then add something else.

"Once we were in a convoy driving through Kabul," said John sleepily. "I was a lookout, and I spot this taxi getting between me and our following vehicle, and we don't like it when anyone gets between us. Then I see these tubes on the front seat that look just like RPGs [rocket propelled grenades], so I draw a bead on the driver and if he had so much as touched those tubes I would have put a few right in his chest."

John closed his eyes, dozed a little, then roused himself and continued.

"We shoot right through the glass in situations like that, because at close range the bullet won't deflect as much. Anyway, it turned out those were just cardboard tubes. I came within a hair of killing him because of cardboard tubes. Things get tense. . . ."

I asked John if he'd rather sleep than talk, and he said there would be time for sleep later and gave my hand a squeeze.

"My record was two hours short of four days straight with no sleep. Twenty-hour days were par for the course sometimes. . . ."

With the relief flooding over, under, and around me came an incredible exhaustion. I lay down next to John and dozed, soothed into dreamless peace by his voice. I woke and John was asleep next to me, his warm shoulder pressing into mine.

12:33 PM. I left John on his bed and went and got Genie. They talked alone for an hour.

John was asleep when Jessica came home. She woke him and they went down to the living room. Then Francis arrived and the siblings were together for the first time in four years. We let them be, even though Ben and Amanda were pestering Genie and me with many a "Can't we see Uncle John *now*?"

Then Jessica's husband, Dani, and the children went into the living room. Moments later I carried in a tray with two bottles of champagne and glasses for everyone.

"To you, John, welcome home!"

John told us about life in the tent city at Bagram, the poverty in Afghanistan, his buddies, how the kids stole stuff out of his pockets, what he could about some of his missions, flying on choppers and military transports hither and yon, firing all sorts of "cool weapons" in the desert, who he'd liked, the experience of briefing generals on several occasions.

Amanda and Ben could not take their eyes off John. Earlier Ben had whispered to Genie, "What shall I say to him?" Now he was smiling and nodding, amazed that this legend talked like a normal mortal, even made jokes.

"Oh, yeah," said John, laughing, "then there was the goat chocolate milk! The contractor bought some 'chocolate milk' from a

Middle Eastern supplier; you know, we flew it in from Qatar or something, and it turned out it was *goat milk*! Okay, so I was working nights and went into the chow hall early and I tried this new chocolate milk. Well, you know, I've had goat milk before, so I knew what it was right away. But on the carton it just said 'milk.' Well, I decided to wait around for the rush later, for breakfast, just to see what would happen. All the guys went for the 'chocolate milk'! I mean, the little cartons looked real enough, even though there was Arabic writing on them. There it was in English for all to see: *CHOCOLATE MILK*. Taste of home! Something we haven't seen on our tray! Damn straight! Okay! All of a sudden you see all these startled-looking guys, you know, most who've never been outside of boot camp or Kansas, wherever, and who have never tasted the, how shall I put it, acquired flavor of goat! And everywhere you look there are about a thousand guys spitting out brown milk and cursing heartily. They all get this really what-the-*hell?* surprised look! And the milk was served up for a week, you know, like we're going to cultivate a taste for this crap because some jackass civilian contractor has this bright idea to cultivate American-Arab friendship or some bullshit, but nobody took it anymore, then it just disappeared. . . . So who knows, maybe they shipped it all to the international peacekeepers, let the Italians take a crack at it!"

John never mentioned any of the close calls we'd heard about in dribs and drabs via e-mail and phone calls and newspaper reports. Maybe he didn't want to scare the kids, maybe he just didn't want to scare us. And nobody asked.

We stood and toasted John, the USMC, and all our men and women in harm's way again. We all clung to John as if he was a life raft. Genie sat with her arm over John's shoulder and the rest of us circled like piranha waiting to dart in and give him friendly shoves, nudges, pats, rub his fuzzy "high-n-tight" haircut, or in the case of the kids, just grab a hand and tug.

John took the kids up to his room. I tagged along and sat in the open doorway and watched them capering around him like a couple of puppies with a big friendly dog. John glanced at me and grinned as he unpacked his "trash."

Soon John's possessions were strewn all over his bedroom floor, along with a fine layer of Afghan sand that crunched underfoot against the old wide floorboards. He held up his Kevlar helmet.

"Ben, these really will stop a bullet, you know, at least sometimes. We had a guy shot at close range with an AK-47 and all he had was a wicked headache and a concussion. . . ."

The kids tried on his helmet and his flak jacket. John demonstrated the gas mask. Then he handed out Afghan and Uzbek money as souvenirs.

A few minutes later John went out for a walk. I offered to go with him but he said he wanted to stroll around the neighborhood alone. "You know, Pop, just to try and get my head in gear."

As the door shut I was overwhelmed by gratitude and also a crushing weight of unexpected sadness. A moment later I was kneeling by my bed. I was praying for Staff Sergeant Shane Kimmett's father, Dan; for Corporal Matthew Commons' mother, dad, and stepmother; for Lieutenant Childers and his parents; and for all the fathers, mothers, sons, daughters, husbands, and wives of those who were not coming home. Before my son went to war I never would have thought of shedding tears as a sacred duty.

———————

Friends came by to pay respects to the returned hero. We ate hamburgers. I wore a bathing suit and T-shirt. It was hot on the screened porch. John was in jeans, looking gaunt, pale under his sandy tan. Once in a while he'd slip away for a smoke. No one knew what to say. There were bursts of chatter then silences.

Francis, as usual, was able to keep the conversation going. I could see he was working to help make this strange day perfect. Jessica was so sweet and hovered over her "little" brother with the same loving tenderness which she bestows on her own children. Genie was smiling and dazed.

John said very little. He was polite to everyone but looked somewhat uncomfortable. There were no more stories. His eyelids were drooping. We ate corn on the cob. More friends came by. John slipped away.

"Bagram to Uzbekistan, to Germany, to Baltimore, then the eight-hour drive . . . no day off since March . . ." I said to no one in particular.

"There will be fireflies tonight," said Genie in a dreamy voice.

There were. Fireflies blinked ghostly green in the tomato patch. It was so humid, my skin was sticky. The whirr of the AC in the distance sounded peaceful.

John is asleep in his room. I've poked my head around his door several times. He's breathing steadily, stretched out on his bed, still dressed. A mound of wrinkled cammies and other "trash" covers the entire floor. Tonight I think even his old DIs would forgive the mess and let him be.

My grandchildren will remember this day the way the old-timers speak of the good old days. John is larger than life to us all, like the country we celebrated tonight with fireworks bursting over the river casting a flickering glow across my son's sleeping face.

50

After church the first Sunday that John was home, he left a file open on my computer for me to read:

The niece and nephew are having a water fight on the back lawn. I can hear the screams of Amanda and Benjamin and women laughing as water flies and summer lives in northern Massachusetts, as it has for as long as I can remember.

Afghanistan is a long ago thing now, despite the fact that I washed the last Bagram and Kabul dust off me just this morning. A water fight on a back lawn is something that has never happened in that country, at least not in a time and place that I can imagine. I was there for four months during one of the most prosperous times that any of the locals remember. Many people still could not afford shoes.

I see Amanda cut a graceful little-girl circle in the lawn as she runs from Benjamin and his water gun. I pray that she and none of her descendents ever see a burka, or taste the dust of wasted, tired land.

51

July 9, 2003

The Sunday roast beef was perfect. Genie was glowing. Jessica, Francis, and John were relaxing. My heart was full of joy for Genie's absolute vindication. Her choice to put her family first, to forgive me so many times, to make this day possible by being our tribe's center, was fully validated in that vivid moment. John talked and we laughed. The starstruck grandchildren were watching him, hovering near, or climbing on him. Genie looked like the beautiful good queen from some fairy tale in the midst of her adoring subjects. I felt as if I were floating, mentally recording the scene as a reminder of what life can be in those moments when love triumphs.

July 12, 2003

6:52 AM. Jessica and the kids are here for another two days. John's trunk arrived. He unpacked it and gave me an inlaid walking stick he bought in a shop in Kabul. My intricately decorated brass-and-bungee-cord Taliban morality police whip is hanging on the knob of my office cupboard, a reminder of an evil my son has risked his life to help stop, and also the source of a few jokes Genie doesn't approve of: "Where's your burka, woman!" or, "Now I finally can keep some order amongst the women of my village!"

52

10:00 AM. John was home for three glorious weeks before returning to his base. One casualty of war was that he broke up with Mollie, his kind girlfriend of three years. It was an amicable, mutual, grown-apart-but-still-friends parting. Another casualty was that he came home smoking more cigarettes than ever.

John went back to his base a week ago. I'm fretting about his smoking. I'm also worried that his breakup will depress him. I'll take that one over worrying about him being shot.

We talked all around the subject of what he did "over there." He says very little. And since I didn't know where the line is between natural reticence and classified information, I didn't press. Did he kill people personally or just help find them? I know he had close calls. I know he speaks of doing bad things to bad people. But he can't or is choosing not to explain further.

Each day since John got home I feel as if gravity has less and less of a hold on me. My mustache is whiter than before John deployed but the dark circles under my eyes are fading. Genie looks ten years younger. I haven't woken up with a jolt for a week. No more nightmares, either.

Genie and I are back to having sex more often, like old times. Our son is no longer at risk. Let's hear it for midday trysts wherein the sole executive of Genie's company indulges in the merciless sexual harassment of her sole employee!

I'm back in the kitchen cooking up a storm and making sure there is plenty of "cooking wine" on hand, i.e., wine to drink while I'm cooking! I realize now that, without planning to, we've been restricting our diets in a sort of perpetual Lenten solidarity with our warrior.

3:29 PM. Jennifer [my friend and literary agent] just called to tell me that she has sold my latest book. My thought was to have this "diary of deployment" be the basis of a nonfiction work on what it's like to be a part of a military family during a time of war. I told Jennifer about my idea a few weeks before John got back home.

"It'll be on their spring list," said Jennifer. "We're committed."

After chatting happily with Jennifer I ran downstairs to tell Genie.

"Great! Congratulations!" Genie said.

I called John at his base and left a message on his cell for him to call back. I called Francis with the good news, then Jessica.

"I think it's great! Well done, Papa!" said Jessica.

"Good. People should know what it's like to go through this," said Francis.

I had asked John's permission to turn this diary into a book. He was enthusiastic. I had also asked him if he wanted to coauthor it like we did with *Keeping Faith*.

"I can't," John had said. "My part is all classified, but I'd like it if you used some of my poems and other pieces I've been sending you."

John has always been my most enthusiastic literary cheerleader. Even when he was a kid he read everything I wrote, was encouraging when I got rejection letters, and rejoiced if I sold something. Before Francis taught me how to use the computer, John would sometimes scribble helpful comments on my first, handwritten drafts.

53

5:10 PM. John called five minutes after I talked to Francis.

"They just agreed to publish my new book!" I told him.

"Oh? Great, Dad," John said quietly. "I was, uh, just about to call you when I got your message."

His tone was unusually subdued. He sounded distracted, not like himself.

"What's up?" I asked. "Don't you like my book idea anymore?"

"No, no, it's not that. I think it's great. No, there's something else. . . . In fact I was about to call you when I got your message, and well, it's sort of weird really, the timing and all. . . ." John paused. I was thinking about the writing work that lay ahead, and wondering why John sounded so flat, suddenly worried he was sinking into some sort of postdeployment depression.

"Dad, I don't want to rain on your parade, but a situation has arisen and it looks like I'll be redeployed next week."

For a moment I didn't understand him.

What? What had he just said? My stomach flipped as the word *redeployed* sank in.

"Right now I'm the most qualified person available to do the job. They need me, Dad."

I was aware of my heart pounding.

"Can they do that? You just got back! I thought that was it!"

"I did too, but things change."

"Did you volunteer again?" I said.

"No."

"Are you telling me the truth?" I said with a forced laugh.

"Not exactly; I did say I'd go when they asked. Okay, I did. You know these intel missions are all volunteer deals."

There was a moment of heavy silence. I just couldn't think what to respond. I was instantly exhausted, proud, resigned, and feeling as if I were sinking through the floor.

"This is my job, what I signed up to do. They need me," said John. "Sorry, Dad," he added quietly.

I responded by shaking my head. I still could not speak. When John broke the silence he tried to cheer me up.

"Anyway, Dad, it'll keep it fresh while you write about what it's like to have a son deployed!"

"Give me a break," I groaned. "Your deployment's 'fresh' enough! It's so damned 'fresh,' I'm still trying to get the ringing out of my ears!"

John chuckled.

"It's not funny!" I said, laughing in spite of everything.

"Yeah, I guess not," said John.

"You sure are one hell of a challenge to keep up with, do you know that?"

"Dad, it won't be any worse than before."

"That was plenty bad!"

"Maybe your writing the book will help you get through it or something, you know, like therapy."

"Fuck the book!" I yelled.

"I know, Dad."

"Therapy?" I roared. "THERAPY?"

"Sorry," said John.

We listened to each other breathing. I heaved another sigh.

"I'm proud of you. When will you know for sure?"

"Monday, by noon."

"You think you're going, don't you?"

"Yes."

"But how can you be ready to go back so fast?"

"You know us, Semper Gumby," said John.

"What?"

"You remember Gumby, 'Always Flexible!' That's us! I have my body armor and cammies and all my trash ready to roll and I probably will be gone by Wednesday."

"Can you tell me where you're headed?"

"Not till I get there. Hey, Dad, isn't it your birthday tomorrow?"

"No. The day after."

"Happy birthday, Dad. How old are you?"

"Forty-nine."

"Bullshit! You've been forty-nine for the last two years!"

"And I plan to be forty-nine again next year too!"

John laughed.

"If I didn't know better I'd say you sound pleased about going out again," I said.

"Yeah, well, it's better than sitting at a desk."

"I like desks," I muttered.

54

August 2, 2003

2:36 AM. I'm less panicked this time. The ache is there but not the raw terror. Is it good to get "used" to your son going to war?

Tuesday, August 5, 2003 8:13 PM
From: John Schaeffer
To: All My Friends
Subj: Bye, Everyone

Well, folks, it's official, I am going back out. It will be the same deal as last time; 3 to 4 months deployed. They asked me last week. I said yes. I was cleared yesterday by the shrinks (imagine that!) and will be headed out circa Friday for places unknown.

Shouldn't be any more dangerous than last time and it's all a crapshoot these days anyhow. I apologize for this mass e-mail, but I just don't have time to write to you all individually. Things are a little hectic right now and I am slightly frazzled. This should be an interesting, if frenetic, deployment and I don't expect anything untoward (no holes, etc.). Maybe I'll see a few of you around Christmas.

All the best,

John

To: Frank Schaeffer
From: Frank Gruber
Tuesday, August 5, 2003 5:41 PM
  Frank,
  Sorry your birthday was dreadful. I suspect it's because I didn't pray for you to have a happy birthday—maybe that was the problem! But you and Genie should be rational enough to expect you're going to fight in the few days after learning John is going overseas again, so stop it. I'm sure she's in the right, anyway.
  Frank

August 8, 2003

John called at 11:40 AM
  "I'm off to the airport," he said calmly.
  We had wanted to go down to DC and say good-bye, but John said no. He said he didn't want to make a "big deal" out of it. "Hey, it's only another deployment, same as before, and I've just seen you for three weeks."

I didn't cry this time. The pain is less a raw gash, more of a deep bruise. I'm fortunate; my son came home alive. I hope and pray that he comes back again. Gregory Commons, father of Corporal Matthew Commons, has other hopes that put my anxiety in perspective. He told me that one day he wants to visit the mountaintop at Takur Gar in Afghanistan. "Someday I hope to run the dirt through my fingers where Matthew died." Matthew wanted to continue college when he got out of the Army, become a teacher like his father.
  I spoke with Lieutenant (Therrel) Shane Childers' mother, Judy

Childers. She said, "I just take it one hour at a time." The fact that I'd called her out of the blue didn't surprise her. She had received many calls, she said. Her steady, quiet voice calmed me. Judy talked about her boy and I listened. She said she was proud of Lieutenant Childers. A few days before he was killed, and in reaction to reading an antiwar newspaper opinion piece—wherein it was claimed that there was "nothing in Iraq worth dying for"—Lieutenant Childers had told his sergeant, "There *are* things worth dying for. Make sure you tell your Marines that!"

Lieutenant Childers wanted to be a rancher in Wyoming alongside his dad, Joe. He was gunned down standing between an onrushing vehicle and his men. "He was a Marine lieutenant. They lead from the front and by example," said Judy. Her son would be proud of his mom.

From: Frank Schaeffer
To: All
Saturday, August 8, 2003 4:38 AM
Subject: John Schaeffer redeployed

Dear All: I ask you to once again remember my Marine son, Cpl. John Schaeffer. He has just been redeployed. The long days (and short nights) for John, Genie, and me begin again. As for John, he is in very good spirits. He did not have to go back but volunteered for the mission when asked.

Thank God for all who serve. May they return safely, and may those of us who wait do so with the faith of our sons and daughters.

Frank

————————————————

Friday, August 8, 2003 1:26 PM

A quick note, Sir, to offer our support and prayers for you and your family while John is away, again. He is a truly exceptional young man. . . . Our Marine, Tim, graduates from boot camp a few weeks from today. . . .

We got a 60-second phone call from him Monday to confirm our arrival in San Diego for Family Day & Graduation. He told us, "Hey, I'm done. I made it. I'm a Marine!" My wife, Suzan, started to cry and Tim told her, "Mom, don't start because then I'll start and I don't want to do that right now, I'll see you all in two weeks."

Then the phone call was over. They sure don't mess around.
Thomas M. Torrez

August 9, 2003

2:49 AM. I was reading e-mails from many friends saying they will pray for my son, just as John called.

"Hi, Dad, I'm in Germany," he said, sounding tired.

"How did the flight go?" I asked.

"No problems."

"Do you know how long you'll be laying over before you get transport?"

"No, but I've got to pull some things together so I can get out of here."

"Did you get any rest?" Genie asked in a sleepy voice.

She had just picked up in the bedroom—I was in my office.

"Hey, Mama. I got about three hours of sleep. I feel fine. Gotta go."

"I love you," Genie and I said in unison.

55

August 11, 2003

John called. He is back in Afghanistan. I feel relieved. Dangerous as it is, at least it's familiar to him. He sounded tired but okay, at work at 2:30 AM their time, taking a break, calling me on a satellite phone. He said he slept under a tractor in the back of the C-17 from Germany to Bagram.

August 14, 2003

The Taliban and Al Qaeda are stepping up attacks. The headline in today's *Times* is about fifty people who died in a series of the worst ambushes, bombings, and shootings seen in Afghanistan in months. Genie is trying to make sense out of our lives.

Since John left for his second deployment, we've settled into a weekday routine very similar to how we functioned during his first time away. Frank gets up early to write, anytime from 3 am on. I wake up later, about 6, make my coffee and see what needs to be done in my office next to the kitchen. Midmorning we break for breakfast, then write and work some more.

We're not sleeping well, very lightly most nights. I'm feeling aged inside. I'm hoping I don't look as old as I feel. If John calls, it's automatically a great day.

I used to keep house so well, to fret if I didn't get the dishes done, beds made, laundry put away. I worried the kids might catch a "disorganization bug." I knew I'd have trouble keeping track of the various family members' schedules if the house got chaotic and I let the disorder invade my brain. I've let things go now. The housekeeping just doesn't seem to matter anymore.

I loved having my kids. We had so much fun just fooling around, having supper after a long schoolday, and reading together in the evenings, working on projects, whatever. They were such good company. When I look back at our lives, this time we find ourselves in now is foreshortened, compressed, and speeds off backward into the distance, its own special infinity. . . .

August 18, 2003

In southern Afghanistan five more Afghan policemen were killed yesterday. Their killers slipped back to our "ally," Pakistan. John sends me a piece of writing.

Chief Kerns is up at three this morning to watch a NASCAR race live. He couldn't wait to watch it when it repeats this afternoon. I, having woken up to piss, sit down and listen to him explain the strategy, how new and old tires act differently at 140 mph, the rules, etc. We have a TV in the tent and get AFN (Armed Forces Network), which brings us TV shows and sports. Today we are watching NASCAR. Scott walks past in the gloom, and he mutters to Chief Kerns, just to piss him off: "Cars turning left, cars turning left."

56

11:50 PM. I just got back to the hotel room from Lieutenant Jane Vizzi Blair's long-delayed wedding reception. Once she and Peter got back they wanted their reception in Miami, where Jane's mother lives. I flew down this morning.

The reception was held in a fabulous 1920s villa replete with high ceilings, a wonderful courtyard, beautiful rococo plasterwork, and tile fountains.

Besides a hundred guests of Jane's mother, Jane and Peter invited military friends, including a group of about twelve Marines, all of whom had just returned from deployments in Iraq and Afghanistan and were wearing their dress blues. They formed an honor guard at the entrance to the vine-covered courtyard.

Lieutenants Jane Vizzi Blair and Peter Blair were beautiful. I was stunned. I had gotten used to seeing them in pictures e-mailed from Iraq, wearing dusty shapeless cammies. Who were these strangers, she in a simple strapless ivory gown that made her exquisite, petite figure seem to float a few inches from the turquoise tile floor; he in his dress blues, gloves, and cover, every inch the tall, handsome Marine?

Jane asked me to stand in for her father, who died when she was a teenager. I gave one of the toasts, touched by the honor.

One of the Marines, Peter's best man, is a chopper pilot. He brought his girlfriend, a Navy chopper pilot he met in training. She just got her wings, was about six feet tall, slender, with ash blond hair and a vivacious and intelligent face, and could have stepped from the cover of *Vogue*. A Navy captain was sitting next to me. Next to him was one of Jane's best friends, a male Marine lieutenant. The Navy captain was Hispanic, the Marine lieutenant black, and the female pilot white.

Jane and Peter made sure that all the enlisted Marines were served first, maintaining the Marines' tradition: officers eat after their enlisted men and women, even at a wedding, even when one officer is the bride! The beauty; kindness; and racial, ethnic, and economic diversity of the young military personnel lining up to load their plates made me feel proud to be an American. I felt humbled to be the father of one of their brothers.

The enlisted Marines came from the same platoon. Several of their platoon members were seriously wounded in Iraq. One is still in the hospital in Germany, shot through the face, part of his jaw blown off.

I wish the reception, and all the cheerful, intelligent conversations going on in it, could have been videotaped and shown on every American campus, to young men and women to whom our military is as foreign as the dark side of the moon.

57

September 2, 2003

1:00PM. John called.

"Did I tell you I got shot at by a kid?"

Genie stifled a gasp. My heart started flip-flopping.

"No," Genie and I both said.

"It was weird," said John with a chuckle. "I was out, on a trip, and we hear this shot and turn around and this kid is running away carrying some sort of old gun that looks as if it's from the eighteen hundreds."

"What did you do?" I asked.

"Nothing."

"What!" I exclaimed.

"What do you expect me to do," John answered calmly, "put a bullet between some kid's eyes? Anyway, the gun was some sort of single-shot musket about a hundred years old. If it had been an AK or something, then of course that would have been different. He went round a corner and we weren't about to run into an ambush with five of our people."

"I'm praying for you," I said.

"That's probably why he missed!" John laughed.

"So what are you thinking these days?" Genie asked in a shaky voice, changing the subject. "I mean about what you'll do when you come home again? Are you going to go to school, work for an intel agency—what's your current thinking?"

"I've learned there are some things it's better not to know," said John. "Ignorance is bliss. I have a really twisted view of the world right now. I'm not sure I have the moral flexibility for this job long term. I think when this is over I'm done."

58

7:50 PM. I was watching the moon rise over the river. Genie had gone to the women's group at our church to do her treasurer shtick. A great blue heron had just settled in the top of a pine tree, when the phone rang.

"Hey, Dad."

"John!"

"Hey."

"The paper makes it sound like all hell is breaking loose over there."

"Yeah, I'm pretty much crushed with the work. I got up at five this morning, uh, yesterday morning, that is. Now it's the next day. I've been going twenty hours."

"You hanging in there?" I asked.

"I feel a real sense of well-being," John said, and chuckled.

"What? Are you joking?"

"No. I really do."

"What about all that stuff about moral flexibility?" I asked. "What did you mean?"

"Things happen. You can be glad I'm busy! When we're not busy we go out looking for trouble, make work. For now I'm stuck on base, going twenty-four/seven. I get a friend to bring me ramen noodles and eat while I work, and tell Mom I'm taking my daily vitamin. Everyone else is sick and I'm not. That vitamin is probably the reason. I know what I'm doing now, the second time around, taking a little better care of myself. Hey, Pop, how's your book coming?"

"Fine, but working on it makes me miss you even more."

"Yeah, well, never mind. I'm fine. The work is stacked up to the moon. But we're getting on top of it."

"Good."

"When you hear about the Taliban attacking, you can divide all the numbers by five. The Afghans exaggerate what's going on."

"Really?"

"Yeah, you know, Dad, most of everything you hear is bullshit."

"I guess."

"I love you. Say hi to Mom. I'm sorry I'm not sending more poems, but the shit is really flying here."

59

John e-mails a piece; this one about the fact that he's been "in country" long enough, so getting shot at is just another day at the office. . . .

> The moon is full. We have just gotten word that OP 6 (Observation Post 6) is taking small-arms fire.
>
> Cable leans over to me as some of the newer people talk in scared voices, as if we're going to end up manning the perimeter, fighting to the last man.
>
> Cable mutters under his breath, "I wonder if that fax I sent made it back to the States."
>
> That simple statement, right there, just about sums it all up for him and me. But just in case, we put one in the chamber and go back to what we were doing.

60

September 25, 2003

We have not heard from John for two weeks. Then this:

Thursday, September 25, 2003 8:27 PM
From: John Schaeffer

Dear Mom and Dad: I have learned that the right thing and the necessary thing are not synonymous, rarely are they even in the same ballpark. It's very depressing to see the results of some necessary actions, it's never pure, and there is no purity here. I have started to pray again.

I have realized that without faith there is no hope. I also realize why many Americans and people of privilege everywhere do not pray. But there are some places where faith is the only thing that can make you take the next step. It is the only hope. It is not a choice. It is all there is.

People ignore what they cannot see. They just don't want to know. The truth is too ugly and vicious to comprehend with a mind that knows only comfort and whose greatest hardship has been dealing with "moral questions" like not eating meat, what music to listen to, or what to wear. People back home invent their own hardships when there are no real ones around. I guess they need them to know they are alive. But once you have seen the real hardships of the world everything else is bullshit.

The world is not a good place. People are not good. Individuals can be good, but it is a matter of opportunity and privilege that makes them so. Goodness is not a natural state.

In a natural state a human will kill, and kill not always for necessity, but for convenience as well. The only way that I know I am still me is that I hate that fact; I hate it more than anything I have ever known. Some of what I have had to do here will eat my soul for the rest of my life.

J

61

Friday, September 26, 2003 5:08 AM
From: Frank Schaeffer
To: John Schaeffer
Subj: your letter to us

Dear John: You can count on our love. What you say about prayer is right; it's the natural and the only response to what the world is.

There is a lot of wrong in my life that you don't know about and will never know but that I carry with me. In spite of all that, I can sometimes feel grace.

There have been many periods of my life when I was ready to give up but continued because of my love for you, and wanting to set some sort of example, not let you down. Remember that you, Jessica, and Francis are the light of Genie's and my life.

In your present circumstances we are not counting on you to know what is right all the time. But we are hoping you will always be our son that we love and come home to us. That you can work on.

I too have done things for which I'll always be sorry and, unlike you, have no excuse of wartime necessity. Next time we're in New York together we'll take a stroll through our beloved Metropolitan Museum of Art and you'll see again that war, peace, art, faith, and human creativity have always been inextricably bound up together. The human journey is messy!

The message of art and history is that hope and regret are inseparable. In this sense there is no human progress. The only real progress is individual and can be measured by the change for good in the content of our characters. In this sense the whole of human history is bound up in the content of each individual's character.

The point is to be honest enough to admit who we are, and to see things for what they are as best we can. You are doing that. What more could a father hope for his son?

I am sorry that you have to see and do things that I'll never be able to help you bear. I'm sorry too that because your part in this conflict is secret you will never have the solace of talking certain things out with your mom or me.

Thank you for your service. I love you with all my heart and always will.

Dad

Friday, September 26, 2003 11:54 AM
From: Genie Schaeffer
To: John Schaeffer
Subj: response from Mom

Dearest,

You are very precise in writing about the crappiness of the human condition. Thank you. You are brave and right to articulate the darkness. I would be much more worried for you if you liked war.

You are caught on the big stage. I don't know what you've had to do. But you are paying the price for a paradox: the paradox of having to battle aggression with at least equal, but hopefully more determined and powerful, aggression in order to halt the spread of further aggression. This must feel incredibly futile. But it is necessary.

You are right. Clear moral choices are only possible for the privileged with options: those that have time and leisure to ponder and discuss and make choices according to their means. But there are no guarantees of good results even then.

War is your reality now; killing can go on so long as to seem a natural state. But there is another reality that doesn't end; the longing to stop suffering is also a natural human desire. I don't believe this is a rationalization.

The central paradox of the Christian faith is God's death to redeem His creation from death. The hope is that this ends evil. Ultimately, I believe that God has given everyone the final privilege: the option to behave better. Forgiveness is freely given because of God's love. That is our hope.

I love you and want you home. We will continue to pray for you and love you always. I want angels to comfort you and bring you back safely.

Mom

62

October 17, 2003

Genie and I have not heard from John for what seems like an eternity. I am the most depressed I have been since John was first deployed. I suddenly realize that my worst fears for John are not what is done to him, but rather what may happen inside of him. I have never felt so helpless. We keep rereading his e-mail. We roll John's phrases back and forth looking for resolution.

"He said, 'Some of what I have had to do here will eat my soul for the rest of my life.' I feel so bad for him. . . ."

"But at least he's praying. . . ."

"At least he's talking to us. . . ."

"Experiences that can't be shared. . . ."

"But he wrote us. . . ."

"I'm so sad for him. . . ."

"He's struggling. . . ."

"And yet doing his job. . . ."

"Struggling to not become brutalized. . . ."

" 'The only way that I know I am still me is that I hate that fact'; he's talking about the killing. . . ."

"He said, 'I hate it more than anything I have ever known.' "

"It would be worse if he liked it. . . ."

63

October 18, 2003

1:23 PM. John called. This is his first call since he wrote to us almost a month ago. We have heard nothing from him since then. We have been so worried about his state of mind.

He sounded calm, very much himself. I did not want to steer the conversation. I just wanted to hear him. We talked for almost an hour! It was the first time we'd spoken for longer than ten minutes during either his first or second deployment. He must have kidnapped the satellite phone! We were disconnected several times. He just kept calling back.

John said he was outside his tent in the dark. He said it was cold and there was snow on the mountains, visible in the starlight. His tone was as laid back as when we used to walk up the Plum Island beach at low tide. From time to time I heard him light a cigarette. Genie is in California visiting her recuperating dad. I made notes for her.

"I'm not sure Al Qaeda and the Taliban even have a plan. It's just all killing. They're just killers, plain and simple. Their 'plan' *is* killing!

"I've paid my dues. I can't keep doing this forever. When I get home I'll have to go to church and light a lot of candles as it is. I can't keep doing this. . . .

"Do you know how brutal it is out here, how fucked-up this place is? Do you know what Islam really does to a country? Afghanistan is the worst of everything, a combination of tribalism and radical Islam. You couldn't come up with a worse combination for destroying all hope. . . .

"I have served, and I'm glad. But one war is enough, at least for me. I can't spend my life in this. I could make good money once I'm out of the Corps, if I wanted to get a job as a civilian contractor for one of the intel agencies, but I don't know if I want to. It isn't that I think what we're doing is wrong. It's the right thing, at least most of the time, and necessary. The people we're after are really terrible. They have to be stopped. But I can't do this all my life. I want to go to school now, make a new start. . . .

"I got written up for a Bronze Star. I probably won't get it and certainly don't deserve it, but it was nice to get written up. I got some other medals awarded to me out here that I'll tell you about some-time. When I get home you can read the Bronze Star write-up.

"I think with any luck I'll be home for Thanksgiving; if not, then by Christmas. I'll tell you one thing: I never want to see another gun! The NRA can kiss my ass."

I felt as if a weight that had been crushing me since reading John's brooding e-mail had been lifted from my chest and shoulders. I did not know, nor did I ask, if Genie and my letters had helped. But John's calm, steady voice let me know that somehow he was working it out in his own way. I knew not to press for details.

64

5:33 AM. We have heard nothing from John for another ten days. Angels come to me sometimes. George Duffy is one.

He drove down from Seabrook yesterday afternoon to get a book signed. As his car pulled into the drive I noticed the front license plate was one of those "POW" plates New Hampshire issues. I recognized the dapper eighty-three-year-old gentleman behind the wheel. We had stood in the mildewed gym many times, shoulder to shoulder, cheering on the IC Pelicans. Mr. Duffy is the grandfather of a girl who was in John's eighth-grade class. He stayed for the boys' games, which were usually preceded by the girls' games his granddaughter played in. For a few minutes we talk IC Pelican basketball. Memories flood back. . . .

The water surface is calm and glassy, the whale emerges in slow motion, seems to be breaking free of the earth. I think he'll drop back any minute but he doesn't, he just soars higher till almost his whole body is out of the water. He hangs above the earth. I hold my breath. Finally John comes down with the ball! The "whale" slides back into the water in an explosion of spray.

The Fremont game! He went end to end, drove between Fremont's two biggest players. When John went for the layup, he seemed to come from someplace below the court, like he was erupting out of those tiles! My killer whale breaking free of gravity!

The place stank of pot roast. I mean, why the *hell* did Fremont think it was a good idea to combine their cafeteria with a gym? But for a second, it was big-time basketball!

The ball rolls around the rim, then slowly trickles into the net. Everybody goes apeshit. The clock's down to twenty seconds. The Pelicans are still behind by two points. The big guy from Fremont has the ball. He's charging up the court. Suddenly John is there with his long arm—Coach called it his "chicken arm"—tipping the ball. John steals it, passes it to P.J., who passes to Jerry, who gets the basket and ties up the game. There are only ten seconds left on the clock. Fremont drives to the basket; their big guy goes up for the shot. He misses. The ball bounces out of the hoop. Twenty hands grab for the rebound but John goes up a lot higher! He crashes out of that forest of grasping hands, shoots up higher than the rest. The clock's down to five seconds, maybe four. It's as if I'm looking through a tunnel. John has the ball! The bulbs on the scoreboard over the cafeteria window are shaping terrible numbers; seconds trickle away, 4, 3, 2, John shoots and misses! Then one last time he does his killer whale routine. John goes for the rebound: up, up, and up! He gets it! John shoots before his feet touch the ground, while the buzzer sounds. Everyone's screaming! Nothing but net!

My son.

Genie, Mr. Duffy, and I stood talking. I asked him about his POW plate. I never knew anything about his having been a POW. Or maybe I did know, but ten years ago the fact hardly would have registered.

Mr. Duffy calmly told Genie and me his story. He told it as cheerfully as if he was telling us about a recent vacation.

"Early in the war I was a young officer in the Merchant Marine. A German auxiliary cruiser sank our ship off Cape Town. Of the crew of fifty-eight, forty-seven of us were pulled from the water and taken prisoner. After four weeks on the German ship, a German replenishment vessel appeared and we prisoners were transferred. Unfortunately for us, this supply ship stopped in Java and we were handed over to the Japs.

"Meanwhile, on the home front, the Shipping Administration declared our freighter lost and our crew killed. Our insurance and wages were paid to our next of kin and the books closed. My mother was told I was dead.

"Before the end of 1942, the Japs allowed us to write letters to our families. On the night of April 23, 1943, our letters were broadcast by Radio Tokyo for propaganda purposes, to 'prove' how well they were treating their American prisoners—of course, we'd had to write pretty much what they told us to. Back home, some fellows listening to short-wave sent penny postcards the next morning to each of the families mentioned in our letters. The Japanese had made us read our names and addresses so the people in the U.S. would know our letters were real.

"One man sent his postcard in an envelope—special delivery. On Sunday morning, April 25, that letter arrived at the post office in Newburyport, Massachusetts, and was delivered to my mother, Alice. Unbelievably, it was Easter Sunday, Resurrection Day.

"It was a long time before I got home, though. My mother had grieved for me, but now I was alive, which brought her a new set of worries: her son was in a notorious camp. Nineteen of our crew died in the camp. By the end of the war those of us who survived tallied over eleven hundred days of imprisonment."

Mr. Duffy fell silent. He was staring out the window at the river.

"Thank you for coming by," I said somewhat lamely.

Mr. Duffy smiled, thanked me for signing his book, a present for his granddaughter, who'd gone to John's school, and said, "I'd better be going now."

Genie and I stood watching Mr. Duffy slowly turning his car in our drive.

65

November 5, 2003

A letter from a Marine, Lieutenant Colonel Tim Bailey, arrives with a very recent picture of John. I don't know Lieutenant Colonel Tim Bailey. The letter comes out of the blue. It's a welcome gift.

John is wearing jeans and a T-shirt and a baseball cap pulled low. He stands next to two other men also dressed in civilian clothes, carrying weapons and wearing flak jackets. John has on his dusty black bulletproof vest. He wears mirrored sunglasses and cradles an M-4. A walkie-talkie is strapped to his leg. His 9 mm is at his side. Behind him the rugged, pale brown Afghan mountains rise to a cloudless cobalt sky. Nearby, six or seven helmeted American soldiers are taking up positions. John's expression is composed, stance relaxed.

Genie stares at the picture, shakes her head, and comments: "It's like looking at some stranger. It feels so surreal to know that this is John."

The letter is an act of kindness, proof that Marines watch even each other's parents' backs. On it was written: "I thought you would enjoy this photograph of your son. It was taken at the southern end of the Salang Tunnel, Hindu Kush, Afghanistan. John is a fine Marine and respected throughout the task force."

I repeat the words "respected throughout the task force" to myself as I look at the picture.

November 25, 2003

As I traveled out to California for three book signings I carried that picture of John that Lieutenant Colonel Tim Bailey had sent to us. I look at it often. But now another picture is burned into my mind: Brianna White laughing. She is the one-year-old daughter of Staff Sergeant Aaron White, USMC. Sergeant White died in a helicopter crash in Iraq on May 19, 2003. I met his widow Michele Linn-White at a book signing at the Marine Corps Association bookstore in Camp Pendleton. She sat quietly talking to me about her husband; about how she thought that even if Aaron—as crew chief—had known his chopper was going to crash he still would have chosen to be with his men.

Michele's sweet demeanor reminded me of my daughter, Jessica. We talked for about ten minutes, while Brianna scrambled on and off her mother's lap and played peekaboo with a couple of Marines. Michele didn't complain, sound bitter, or in any way intimate that she thought she deserved more help. Her answers were composed, frank, and without a shred of self-pity. But I learned that Michele was going back to school and she could not afford day care for Brianna. She said neighbors would help out.

As we ended our conversation Brianna was back on her mother's lap. She was smiling brightly, eyes sparkling, a testimony to her mom's love. I think Aaron would have been proud.

In the presence of this bravery I felt undeserving of my life's blessings and humbled that Michele would buy a book about the USMC coauthored by someone who never served and whose only association with the Corps was through his son. Thoughts about John somewhere out in the Afghan desert were almost overwhelming. This lovely mother and her beautiful child had not been spared life's greatest sorrow. There were no guarantees of happy endings. And they had been far more dependent on Aaron than I was on John. . . .

I am not proud of the couldn't-care-less attitude I once harbored about men and women in the military. And I am not proud of the way my rich country sloughs off our military families when we're done with them. I am not proud of the sanctimonious American left that wants "economic justice" for everyone except for our underpaid military and—these days—almost never provides any volunteers. I am not proud of the American right that says it supports our military but makes sure its kids aren't serving.

Just before the signing Jane Vizzi Blair and Peter Blair stopped by. It's the first time I've seen them since Miami. They drove three hours from their base at Twenty Nine Palms and stood nearby as I talked with Michele and signed books. Both are well. Peter is about to be deployed to Okinawa and, in all likelihood, Jane will be sent back to Iraq. So soon after marriage these two are to be separated again, this time for at least nine months, maybe a year. After the signing we grabbed a quick lunch on base.

"I remember that chopper crash," Jane said, and shook her head.

"I think six Marines were killed," said Peter. "It wasn't too far from where I was."

We ate in silence.

"The 9/11 victims' families were taken care of but not the military families who lose someone," said Jane quietly.

"Until Dan Kimmett—the father of a killed Air Force special ops guy—set me straight, I always thought military widows and orphans got big settlements and life-long benefits or something," I said.

Jane shook her head. Her eyes were wide with annoyance.

"It's *disgusting* how the families get treated."

"And it's just as bad for the wounded and disabled," said Peter. "There are all these voluntary groups for veterans because the government doesn't do enough."

"Michele will only get some mostly short-term benefits that amount to a handful of glorified food stamps," said Jane. "As I said, compare that to the millions that went to each 9/11 family. What about a Marine's family after he lays down his life for his country?" [See Appendix.]

After lunch I left for another book signing, this time for *Zermatt*, at Dutton's, located in L.A.'s swanky Brentwood neighborhood. Perhaps, I thought as I sped up the freeway, when the burden of military service was shared fairly between all classes of Americans— before Vietnam and "student deferments," not to mention the all-volunteer military—the stinginess of the benefits paid to surviving families might have been acceptable. At least back then, everyone did their bit. And maybe when we fought wars wherein tens of thousands were killed and maimed we couldn't afford to be generous. But since Vietnam our wars have been relatively "low casualty." Our nation has become wealthier than ever and our craven elites have opted out of service and left the fighting, the being maimed, and the dying to a few patriotic Americans.

November 26, 2003

I stayed with Frank Gruber after my signing in Brentwood. He was solicitous about John but something seemed to separate me from the good cheer, hospitality, and conversation. I had never before been so aware of the vast gulf that divides those who serve and those, like Frank and me, who benefit from that service. I can't get Michele and Brianna out of my mind.

"Some military widows might also qualify for a Social Security benefit, but not all," I said to Frank.

He looked at me a bit blankly. A somewhat embarrassed silence followed. Where had this come from?

"A widow gets a form condolence letter and six thousand dollars. In Michele's case the form letters came from the President and Congress with her name spelled wrong," I said.

While I watched Frank open another bottle of fine red wine to freshen our glasses, I couldn't help wondering about enjoying the "good life" in a country that takes for granted that some Americans do all the sacrificing while the rest of us act as if we deserve a life without hardship.

November 27, 2003. Thanksgiving

I met Genie yesterday in Oakland and drove up to Pam's [Genie's sister] home in Napa. John was to have been with us for Thanksgiving, if he hadn't had his second tour unexpectedly extended.

Everything was wonderful but I missed John horribly, and I felt like I was stealing from somebody. The only people in the room who seemed to me to have earned the good time we were all having were Genie's mom and dad and her brother Tom. Genie's parents both served in WWII and Tom served in the Army in the Vietnam era.

66

John may have volunteered, but I was drafted. We have an all-volunteer military, but we, the platoon of parents, wives, children, and husbands of those who serve, are given only one choice: to love or not. Our job is to struggle with our fears in plain sight of the carefree lives we used to live, and in plain sight of our friends and leaders who have no direct involvement; no loved ones at risk . . . no skin in the game.

As somebody who never used to notice POW license plates, I deserve having been "drafted"! The Greek Orthodox monks say that struggle purifies the soul. I hope so. Genie wrote:

> *A couple of days after John got home from his first deployment, I told him about my dad's illness. Dad was still in treatment at the time and too tired for visitors. But John called him and they had a good chat. I was hoping John could see my father when his treatment was done but John shipped out again before that could happen.*
>
> *I saw my parents at Thanksgiving last week. They are as lovely as ever. Dad's treatment went well. Mom is fine too. Dad is eighty-six years old and Mom is eighty-four. My parents haven't seen John for five years. A lot has happened in that time.*
>
> *We're hoping John will be home from his second deployment in time for Christmas, when we'll try again to get together, this*

time in California. It might only be for three days, but my par-
ents and family understand how it is; you don't have to explain
anything to them—my mom and dad both were in World War
II. We hope the visit happens, but if it doesn't we'll be strong
because that is what life requires, especially the military life. I
now know that through all the uncertainties, you make a plan;
you stay strong and hope for the best.

After John got back from his first deployment I told him that
one of my concerns was his youth ending so abruptly. "Is your
childhood over?" I asked.

"Yup, it's gone," John answered.

I knew what he said was true. Our son was the same but
changed. I don't expect to know how changed for quite a while.

There are Americans who love John and are praying for him even
though they never met him. Some have faced war. And they are
not the people I've spent my life clawing to get next to, "useful con-
tacts" a writer needs to know. My angels are more likely to be men,
women, and children with whom I have nothing in common except
that we share a single heart.

Some Americans will sleep rough tonight so I can sleep securely
in my comfortable bed. One of them is my son.

My illusion of independence is gone. Being a privileged American, living in the twenty-first century, has not saved me from a small
taste of the emotions that Mrs. Duffy felt in 1942, or that some
Greek father, living in 480 B.C., experienced when his son went to
war against the army of Xerxes. Mrs. Duffy and that forgotten father
seem to be murmuring, "For better or worse this is the price of
freedom. Welcome to the human race."

Maybe someday Genie and I will know how war changed our
son. For now all I know is that, like John, my childhood is over.

Postscript

Saturday, November 22, 2003 1:29 PM
From: John Schaeffer, USMC
To: All

Hey, if you see anything on the news or in the paper about a bad chopper crash here, I'm fine. I'm not exactly sure how to tell you this, so I'm just going to tell you, I've been extended—again—until the middle of next month. Sorry, no return for Thanksgiving. It's just the way the dice fell out. However, I can tell you 100% for sure proof positive that I will be out of here no later than 15 December, meaning that I will make it home in time for Christmas, which is nice. I don't have time to write more. I am a little busier than most of the western world combined at this point, sorry to everyone, I am fine and safe.

  love,

  John

Friday, December 12, 2003 12:01 PM
Subj: Christmas Dates
From: Mom
To: John USMC

Hey, sweetie, sorry I missed your call; but I'm glad you and Dad had a good talk.

Dad and I discussed various ways of having Christmas if you make it back in time. All options are fine with us.

Options are:

1) You come home.

2) We come to your base.

3) We postpone Christmas festivities until a better time if you can't make it.

The choice is yours depending on when you get back and what kind of time you can take off. If you get a 96 [ninety-six-hour pass], that's 4 days including the weekend, right?

Christmas Day is on a Thursday; I could book you a ticket up here for Christmas morning, going back on Sunday. Or you maybe could fly up on Friday and back on Monday. Or we can drive down.

So let me know what it looks like, as I should book tickets soon. Any tickets would be refundable in case plans change, so don't worry about it.

And don't stress if you don't know what to do now; we can wait and figure it out together later, after you're back and talk to the powers that be. Christmas will be whenever you are with us even if it's May! So don't worry, you won't miss anything.

Love,

Mom

Monday, December 12, 2003 10:57 PM
From: John Schaeffer, USMC
To: All

Hey guys, Sorry if some of the typing comes out a little weird. I had to beat this computer [in Uzbekistan where John was traveling—FS] into using English characters. I probably screwed something up, so if it comes out that there are weird characters mixed in I apologize. Should be getting back tomorrow evening, that's 17 December, Wed. Not Tuesday, which at this point I think is tomorrow for you folks. No holes, doing fine, tired.

See you later.

J

December 18, 2003

John called last night at 9 PM. He is on U.S. soil! He called from the pay phone in his barracks. He sounded tired and annoyed. Genie and I did not know when he'd get in and had been waiting by the phone all day.

"I'm so pissed off," said John with a sigh.

"Why?" asked Genie and me in unison.

"The idiots decided to do some work in our barracks while I was gone, took all my books, clothes, and possessions and tossed them in a pile on the floor and removed the furniture from my room. I don't have a locker or bed. A thousand dollars' worth of uniforms, my suit, everything I own, is balled up in a corner and covered in dust. I can't find my cell phone. I can't find anything. I had everything dry-cleaned just before I left. There's a hole where the shower used to be. I have no bed, the place is a wreck."

"A homecoming fit for a hero," I said.

"Yeah," answered John.

"*Hey*, WELCOME HOME!" I yelled.

"Yes!" said Genie.

"I'm glad to be back, glad and tired." John yawned. "Now if I can just find a place to take a shower. . . ."

"Major Hartman wrote you a lovely letter of recommendation to the colleges you're applying to," said Genie.

"That's great," John said, brightening.

"Get some rest and we'll talk about Christmas plans tomorrow," said Genie.

"We can't wait to see you," I said. "Go to a hotel tonight and I'll pay for it, get a good night's rest."

"Nah, I'll just sleep on the floor. No big deal, but I can tell you one thing: the Navy idiots who run this barracks can damn well spring for my cleaning bill!"

December 19, 2003. [Final Entry]

John called at about noon. He sounded cheerful.

"So, what happened with the room?" I asked. "Who did this to you, the Marines or the Navy?"

"Both!" John laughed. "It takes two major services' best efforts to screw over a Marine this bad! But they said they'll pay for the dry cleaning. So it's okay. Plus I found my cell phone."

"How's the car?" I asked.

"Steve's coming over to give me a jump. The battery's dead. I don't know what shape it's in."

"What about Christmas?" Genie asked.

"I should know in a day or two," said John.

The nation that makes a great distinction between its scholars and its warriors will have its thinking done by cowards and its fighting done by fools.

—Thucydides

Appendix

According to the *New York Times,* an average of $1.8 million per 9/11 victim was paid out by the U.S. government to their families. Compensation for injuries went to 3,440 people, with individual awards of up to $7.9 million. A total of $3 billion was paid by the government to the injured and to the surviving families. Those who signed up for the payout agreed to waive their right to sue the airlines whose planes were hijacked, thus protecting both the airlines and the insurance companies.

When an American in uniform is killed, his or her family receives a one-time "death gratuity" of $6,000. (In 2004 this was increased to $12,000.) The surviving family may also qualify for the "Survivors Benefit Plan" (SBP), paid up to age sixty-two or until the widow(er) remarries. SBP amounts to 55% of the soldier's retirement pay, which itself is calculated against a percentage of pay so low it already qualifies some military families for food stamps. Michele did not qualify for this because Aaron was in the Corps *just under 10 years.* Several further benefits, like the income-based Dependency and Indemnity Compensation (DIC), run by the VA, *may or may not* pay out about $800 to the surviving spouse per month and $200 per child per month, depending on the case. Again, Michele did not qualify. Medical benefits continue for three years, then end. (If the soldier, sailor, Marine, Coast Guard, or airman has "Service Members Group Life Insurance" (SGLI) they receive a life insurance payout. But not all service members pay for this strictly optional insurance.)

Acknowledgments

My Marine son, Corporal John Schaeffer, is the inspiration for this book. Moreover, he contributed a number of poems, letters, and prose pieces to it. A simple "thank you" is hardly adequate, but thank you, John. And thank you for your service.

My beloved wife of thirty-three years, Genie, is my first reader, and first editor. She also contributed several passages to this book. Thank you. Jessica and Francis are loyal friends, and a wonderful daughter and son who make life worth living. They give good advice on all my writing projects and are a tremendous encouragement. They allowed me to use things they said and wrote herein. Thank you both.

My agent, Jennifer Lyons, is my friend and champion. Thank you. My editor, Will Balliett, makes my writing much better; his friendship and support breathed life into this project. Blanca Oliviery's endless effort and creativity in promoting *Keeping Faith* (and kindness to its authors) helped pave the way. Thank you Peggy McPartland for a deft copy edit and Joni Vetne for her help.

I want to thank my old and dear friend Frank Gruber for allowing me to use some of our correspondence herein, and for his excellent editorial advice on this and all my projects. I am grateful to Captain George Duffy (US Merchant Marine, Ret.) for his generously allowing me to retell his story and for checking my brief account for accuracy. Unless otherwise attributed, newspaper headlines used in the text are from the *New York Times*.

Above all, I want to thank the families of military personnel, the former military personnel, and the active duty military men and women who kindly gave me permission to print their letters. In recognition of my correspondents' abundant generosity, a portion of the publisher's and author's income from this book will be donated to the Military Child Education Coalition.

The Military Child Education Coalition (MCEC) works to make educational opportunities a reality for the children of the men and women in our armed forces. MCEC also provides help to military families in settling into the new communities to which they are moved. Donations or inquiries may be made online or sent to:

Military Child Education Coalition
108 E. FM 2410, Suite D
Harker Heights, TX 76548-2519
www.militarychild.org

FRANK SCHAEFFER
January 10, 2004
www.frankschaeffer.com